LET GO OF THE SH*!
OF THE
SHOW

{ Conquer Your
"SUCCESSFUL DISCONTENT"
and Live Free and Fulfilled }

MICHAEL R. VUKELIC

Let Go of the Shit Show
Conquer Your "Successful Discontent" And Live Free And Fulfilled

Edited by: Danne Reed
Cover Designed by: Kendra Cagle
Book Interior Designed by: Kendra Cagle

ISBN: 978-0-578-66196-4

Additional books by Michael Vukelic may be purchased at:
OutrageousSuccess.com

Outrageous Success
400 Washington Street
Northfield, MN 55057

{ DEDICATION }

* * *

I dedicate this book with heartfelt thanks
to my amazing teachers, mentors and masters.

TABLE OF CONTENTS

* * *

Acknowledgements i

Foreword By Linda Williamson iii

Prologue. vii

CHAPTER 1 Life is Wonderful... and Then It Isn't. 1

CHAPTER 2 The Successful Life 9

CHAPTER 3 The Beginnings. 17

CHAPTER 4 Build It and It Will Come 23

CHAPTER 5 The Discovery: We Are Not Who
We Believe We Are 39

CHAPTER 6 Seeking and Asking 49

CHAPTER 7 The Basics: Science and Spirituality 61

CHAPTER 8 The Separate Self Identity. 69

CHAPTER 9 Love Thyself. 93

CHAPTER 10 Define Your End Results 109

CHAPTER 11 How We Sabotage Our Own Joy 129

Epilogue: Coming Home. 147

{ ACKNOWLEDGEMENTS }

***

I wish to acknowledge my beautiful family. My Mom and Dad, whose guidance and teachings have led me on a perfect journey of learning and growth I would never have experienced without them. To my siblings, for providing opportunities and examples for deeper understanding of the human condition and ways to flourish in a challenging world. It is from my family that I learned some of the most important lessons of life.

To the childhood friends and loved ones who have influenced my life in so many ways, the men who stood by my side in the military, the co-workers at corporations and all the amazing Loves, Guides and Souls; you have touched my life deeply. Thank you all for the role you played in my life. You are all my teachers and I trust you appreciate the teacher I have been for you.

A big thank you to Danne Reed, my editor who encouraged me to finish this project, and my Graphics artist Kendra Cagle. Thank you both for your creativity and expertise in making this dream come to life.

Most importantly, to Cindy who has become a mirror of my every thought, belief and story, I am blessed to learn and continue to learn from your amazing sunshine.

} FOREWORD {
By Linda Williamson

* * *

As Michael releases this book, we are here in the midst of the Covid-19 pandemic - an historical event of epic proportions. A time of change like none other over the past century! A representation that the world is evolving! Humans are progressing toward increased awareness of their real purpose and new avenues to be "whole" and "live alive" in service to all. This book creates new ways to perceive and believe in ourselves! With the world changing rapidly, we must begin to change with it: as many of the old ideas of life are being challenged.

I was delighted and honored when I received the request from Michael to write the forward introducing his book! But I am even more delighted for all who will read it, to have the benefit of his wisdom and selfless sharing of his life experience! What he offers us specifically is the empowerment to breakthrough our old paradigms, live fully and get the most from our lives! It is an invitation to understand and harness our personal power!

Yes, we all have flaws, have made mistakes, had troubles and problems... Yes, we may have been stuck here for some time, even a long time! But Michael succeeds in keeping our focus on the change available: change that guides us to where we want to be! Allowing us the power and perception to transform ourselves now! - In proportion to the level we are ready and willing to give up the sh*! show...

I met Michael when he came to me to be certified in hypnosis by the National Guild of Hypnotists as a Certified Consulting Hypnotist. He had certainly experienced considerable success (by society's standards) in the corporate professional world, however, he also experienced patterns of *discontent, disappointment and discomfort*. This was the "Sh*! Show" he was determined to understand and let go of. Moreover, he brought to the training an enormous, genuine curiosity of who we really are and how we are creating our lives! How our consciousness and subconsciousness are working together for us. He mixed these perspectives in with additional certifications that he achieved along his perfect journey: Holistic Life Counselor, Certified in HMR, (Holographic Memory Resolution) through Brent Baum and became a Certified Trainer through Jack Canfield for Success!

People are drawn to these kinds of answers because the wisdom of the information itself (unlocked from fields of Neuroscience, Physics and messages offered from Enlightened Spiritual Masters) is so very freeing and powerful! Michael understands from his own triumphs that the true integration of higher knowledge to rise above our challenges can be done. I am so appreciative to Michael (and you will soon be as well!) for his willingness to document the details of his journey, including how he developed that courage for change. This is a courage we each need to cultivate. And he offers the processes in great detail as he demonstrates steps that can be accomplished by even a novice in self-empowerment.

Many of us follow our conditioning from parents, society, religion and friends - and wind up creating a conditioned life rather than our own heart's desire. To convey the importance of breaking free from that conditioning, this book explains in detail what Michael did to break free! Which ANY OF US can achieve and it is never as hard as our Ego belief system makes it seem!

We are opened, as we connect with his words, to recognizing who we really are! Which helps create some deeply needed peace in our lives! Knowing our own power and ability to have a life we desire, fulfilled and free, without clinging to the old beliefs and ideas of success is brilliant! It is currently time for all of humanity to realize that synching our mind with our heart's desire is powerful! Using our own power through visualization, guided imagery, and our higher mind is more important today than ever. Taking inspired action from this energy? This is where our power lies; Right Here! Right Now!

Here Michael has put together the teachings and guidance that he sought out and benefited from over the past 15+ years. His book contains unique tools and understandings that assisted his life-changing shift from living from his old automatic conditioned responses of life to living life freely and feeling alive! This is so important today because life is complicated! Michael's clear, understandable answers enlighten us on this journey! And he delivers by showing you how to *Let Go of Your Sh*! Show!*

So, get ready and let go!

Linda Williamson

Certified Hypnotist and Certified Instructor of Hypnotists,
Mid-America Hypnosis Conference Hypnotist of the Year 2007
2017 Order of Braid of Hypnotists through National Guild of Hypnotists

PROLOGUE

* * *

How did I get here? Why am I writing this book? Who am I to tell you anything that can rock your life? Because I lived it. I am still living it. I have made the journey beyond *"Successful Discontent"* and the associated disappointment, discouragement, and depression to joy, love, and success. It truly is like living in another dimension. It is now my life's work to guide others on their own journey. To use their mind and their muscle to create their own miracles, to find true peace and joy, and transform their experience. This book is the beginning of your journey. The pages that follow contain evolutionary wisdom and knowledge that will support and encourage you to realize your real potential and your extraordinary self, which will catapult your life in the direction you have always wanted to go.

Having become very successful by society's rules, I have experienced many great moments of success at work, in my relationships, and financially. But throughout my life experience, there was always a price to pay or an upheaval of sorts in the pursuit of my dream. Many a great moment would be thwarted somehow, by an event that left me discontent or unhappy. Uncomfortable conversations or unpleasant situations that over time would cause great disappointment, discouragement, and even depression. Through this work, I now have the ability to break free from this bondage and it is my mission to support you to do the same.

This book will awaken you. It will reveal the infinite possibilities of your life. Whether you are aware of this or not, you have been trained to see yourself, the world and the possibilities of your life through conditioning: generations and generations of the same thoughts and perspectives. Compared to the possibilities for your life, you have been programmed to think small, even minuscule in the scheme of things. It's time to understand the real meaning of your life, why you are having this experience and how powerful you are, in your adventure to living fully.

We will discuss what science has discovered about your thoughts, and how your thoughts affect your biology, and your life experience. And how predominant thought and state of mind become addictive and difficult to break free of, creating a fear of change.

We will also learn Metaphysical and Spiritual evolutionary wisdom. Wisdom that facilitates an awakening to a new perspective of ourselves and our experience. Perfecting and cultivating an understanding that life is a perfect journey toward growth and higher knowledge. New knowledge that leads us to discover our joy, our state of empowerment and a renewed connection to our soul.

Through the processes contained within, this book will connect you to your life and give you the tools and knowledge to become joyful as never before. There is a profound peace in knowing how magnificent you are. And from that magnificent place of peace, grows a new you, enabled to be authentic, successful, and free.

Enjoy and feel
EACH PAGE
on your
ADVENTURE
to
FREEDOM, FULFILLMENT, & JOY!

***

CHAPTER 1

LIFE *is* WONDERFUL... *and then* IT ISN'T

Have you been there? Everything is beautiful and then it's not? Life is good and then it's back to discontent? A pattern of doubt, fear, upset and then self-judgment? I certainly was in that vicious cycle, but eventually I started to notice the pattern. I began to get curious. I asked, "Why is this happening?" and wondered, "Will it ever stop?" But I am getting ahead of myself here.

For a large part of my life, I convinced myself that my life was good and I *was* happy. Ingrained from my upbringing, I believed the ups and downs were a normal part of life. I spent my income and my time traveling, exploring a new experience or finding a new sweetheart to create temporary enjoyment, but always came back to a feeling of the doldrums and feeling dissatisfied and disappointed. Through a lack of understanding regarding life and myself, I experienced confusion that eventually led to a feeling of hopelessness. I've met a lot of people who have experienced the same.

The fact was... I did not love my life.

Can you honestly say that you love your life? Do you have outward measures of success, but on the inside feel adrift? On the outside looking in, I appeared to have had it made. Some days I felt accepting of my life, but much of the time, there was a nagging feeling that this was not really how life was supposed to be.

One day, feeling exhausted and confused from my repeated efforts and attempts to create situations and events that I thought would make me happy, the pain became too great. I did not know if I could continue.

I boldly began to ask what in the world do I need to know? I stopped filling my life with distractions that caused temporary happiness. I became extremely curious.

Are you feeling curious? Ready to wake up? Do you want to let go of temporary happiness and find the real thing?

At some point in life many of us come to the conclusion that something doesn't add up and life needs to change. An aha moment. A realization that there is more. Sometimes it shows up as an explosion, sometimes it is a launch. Sometimes we sit in it for a lifetime and quietly fade away.

I didn't want to just fade away. I asked and prayed and asked and prayed to be shown how to create and embrace a life of true joy. I asked how to connect with people in a profound way, to live with passion and purpose and turn my life around.

My journey led me to the conclusion that all I had learned, all I had taken as truth — the "truth" that would make me successful and happy — wasn't what would make me happy at all. This striving for something to make me happy became exhausting and was not the answer.

*I knew there had to be a **different Truth.***

What I have learned from 17 years of higher uncommon knowledge and through the subsequent awareness and healing that has occurred, is nothing less than extraordinary. The day I stepped away from what I thought I "should be" triggered a chain of events, and opened new doors, which gave me the chance to live fully and completely, without regard for my past. A real awakening has occurred in my life.

This is the story of how I got here and my sincere wish that it supports you in achieving your dreams. My mission is to share this with everyone who may be struggling in any area of their life. May you hear the higher truth and take the steps to change.

***

SUCCESS AND CONFUSION

Maybe you are successful in the eyes of the world, like I was. Maybe, like I did, you also find yourself returning to feelings of dissatisfaction and unfulfillment no matter what you accomplish. Maybe you are confused as to how you seemingly have it all, yet still feel like something is missing. I wondered that too. The reason is, as with most people, I allowed my Ego to run the show. The Ego — an identity created from the beliefs, patterns and stories of the mind — is that part of us that is never fully satisfied, never totally happy and always wants more. It may seem like the most important and most powerful part of us, as it can wreak havoc on your life, but the Ego is quite insignificant and weak. Every concept, perception, state of mind, belief, and reaction create the Ego self. The Ego, or as I call it, "The Separate Self," believes in separation and forms an identity that lives in fear. If this topic is new to you, stay tuned. I will dissect the notion of the Ego and how I came face to face with understanding and working with this conditioned part of me to find true happiness.

I've always been really curious about life. I mean, I asked myself a lot of questions. Ever since I was a young child I questioned everything. Questions like, what is life really all about? Is there a point? What am I really doing here? Why does my learning in Catechism not add up or make sense? Am I just having an experience — I get born, I die, it's over?

Without real awareness, these types of questions set me out on a journey that is nothing less than incredible, awesome and astonishing! I've learned so much from this life experience, so much from family, people, friends, careers, adventures. Most of all, I learned how perfect it is.

I have learned to understand why we are here! How this world works! How we work! This is what I want to share with you: my journey, the wisdom I *asked* for and have *been given,* and the amazing adventure that followed.

ARE YOU
READY
for your own
ADVENTURE?

- *If you're troubled by a nagging feeling that "this is not how life is supposed to be", listen up and take heart! That nagging feeling is your authentic self, ie: the soul, trying to get your attention!*

- *Foster your sense of curiosity. It's the first step in making meaningful changes in your life.*

- *If you're feeling exhausted by the "striving" to be happy, you're in luck! There is a better way, and I'll show you how!*

- *The Ego Self is an identity created from the beliefs, patterns and stories of the mind. It is that part of us that is never really satisfied, never totally happy and always wants more. And it can be mastered.*

- *Through the learning that I'll share in this book, you'll be able to embark on your own incredible, astonishing adventure of life!*

See Workbook for
Activities and Exercises

{ CHAPTER 2 }

* * *

The
SUCCESSFUL
LIFE

It's another day, or night, depending how you look at it. I am just waking up, my thoughts are jumbled. Oh yes, it's dark outside; it's about ten o'clock at night and the start of my day... I think? I wake and stumble out of bed just in time to grab some leftovers and watch my wife go to sleep. Did I remember to give her a kiss? I don't know. I hope so. Yes, this is the start of my day.

Exhaustion. Confusion. Discontent.

I think back to my days in college, gaining an education to do this work, I never thought I would be here. In college it was all fun. I had the idea of the big-time job, the wonderful income, all the benefits and my successful life. Being able to help my parents, to live abundantly, differently than I was raised — that was my dream. And with focus and effort that dream did become my reality... with a few unexpected twists.

This day my life is strained. My marriage is pushed to its limit and what I have to show for it is a big bank account, horrible bags under my eyes, and suffering. Life has become painful. It's been more than ten years since I have slept well. I have learned that being around family and friends is important. But I work nights, have Tuesdays and Wednesdays off, and rarely see friends. Or family. Or my wife.

What have I learned from my unique vantage point today? I could have changed any of this the moment I decided to. But this night, like so many nights before it, I continue to trudge into work at 11 PM and resentfully travel home at 7 AM each day. Exhausted. Confused. And Discontent.

What I don't see this day is that this is all my choice. This is my so-called "dream", and the irritation and resentment of living it is beginning to show up in my work, in my friendships, in my marriage and in my health. I do my best to convince myself that this is the way it supposed to be. To show up with a smile. I have a great job and a great income, and I've acquired many beautiful things. Many, many beautiful things and many benefits most people will never enjoy.

I can't stop myself from wondering...
**What is going on here? How can I be upset
with this "dream" life?**

I can't stop the next question either...
Is this my dream? Is this what I really want?

When I think back to my childhood and how hard it was for my parents, how they struggled to make house payments, and to feed, clothe and take care of their children, I'm caught in a conundrum. I've reached for a different life and achieved it; made sacrifices and attained my goals. How could I possibly want out? What would I do? What would that mean? What would people think? And what about all the things I have attained?

But then comes the thought — *I deserve to be angry.* This isn't what I was told this career would be. I had no idea I would be working nights, not able to attend a holiday get together and rarely seeing my friends or my wife. And I had no idea this work would be miserable for me. Now that I'm here what do I do? This company upsets me. My life upsets me. I upset myself. None of the options seem right.

Yet the questions continue. If I leave how do I make my house payments? Wow, I would most likely lose the house. What about raising a family? Not sure that will even happen anymore. I don't feel as close to the wife these days. What about traveling? We do both love to travel. And the pay is good.

This whole situation has got me upset! Why am I dealing with this? Where did the fun go?

Just then my mind says: "Mike, you must suck it up and get to work!"

To which I reply: "But I am so miserable and unhappy, is that how I should feel?"

My patterned mind: "Many people feel that way; it's the price you must pay to earn a great income!"

Then my heart attempts to get in on the conversation: "Michael, if you leave it will all work out, and you will be..."

My mind rudely interrupts my heart: "You better get to work; you're late!"

After which... I jump in the car and hurry off to work.

And my heart dies a little.

Each day that passes I become more aggressive as I drive, more isolated when I am at home, and less satisfied with my life and career. I am somewhere between fear, confusion and depression, and each time I feel as though I attain some clarity or a way out of this mess, I get pulled back in by the thought - "It will be okay; just keep working. You're getting a raise soon, and your buddy Jim has a birthday party tomorrow."

Somehow, I convince myself it is okay to stay, to keep living this way, to just make the best of it.

The idea that I am doing so much better than most people, the fear and lack of trust in my ability to create the life I really want, combined with the horror of what I might lose if I make a new or different choice has got me smack in the middle of confusion, stuckness and "Successful Discontent!"

The living of life from someone else's idea of what life should be is not working and my talents are stifled in mediocrity.

How did I get here?

ACTUALLY...
it was
PRETTY EASY!

- *You do NOT have to live a life of exhaustion, confusion or discontent. There is a better life out there for you. Don't settle for less than you desire.*

- *Often, our concept of how life "should" be is formed in childhood, and is based on seeing what we DON'T want, and simply creating the opposite. These concepts are rarely the path to true happiness and contentment in life.*

- *The pressure to feel grateful for what you have and not need more can sometimes work against you in your journey to happiness.*

- *In order to move beyond Successful Discontent, you'll have to move through some fairly powerful fears, but your amazing life is waiting on the other side!*

⇩

See Workbook for
Activities and Exercises

{ CHAPTER 3 }

***

The BEGINNINGS

I was raised in little town, USA, a river town west of Chicago. We lived in a small home. My dad was in the military for more than 34 years and my mom was at home raising us. We didn't have much money. Friday was Beeny-Weiny Night. If you're not familiar with the delicacy, that's chopped hot dogs mixed with canned beans.

Like any other child, I learned from watching and listening to my parents. I took in and believed the many things they said to me and *about* me. My experiences with them and throughout life became learned patterns of behavior and belief systems; what to fear and what to accept. Through their perception of life, work, money, God, women, men, children, and most importantly, their perception of me, I was molded and programmed. What all of society, adults, teachers and friends felt and believed were true and important, with good intention, became a large portion of my values and how I perceived and operated in the world.

My curiosity as a child was eventually replaced by a sense of conformity as my mind integrated *their* truth. That's how it works with most of us. We stop questioning and accept what is around us to be true. Ah, but here is the kicker - 99% of this information is absolutely NOT true!

***

HERE ARE A FEW OF THE THINGS I CAME TO BELIEVE FROM MY UPBRINGING.

- *You must work hard to be successful.*
- *Be nice to everyone, it's just the right thing to do.*
- *Get angry when you don't get what you want.*
- *Money does not grow on trees.*
- *Watch what you do because what will the neighbors think!*
- *You did not do that right.*
- *You are handsome.*
- *God is angry when we sin and we will go to hell for our sins.*
- *Stop crying or I will give you something to cry about.*
- *Everything is expensive.*
- *Love doesn't work very well.*

- *You are smart.*
- *Make lots of money and you won't have to live like this.*
- *Life is hard.*
- *People are mean.*
- *God is always watching us and will punish you if you do something wrong.*
- *Help Mom when she is discouraged or sad.*
- *You are a good kid.*
- *Keep quiet and have fear when Dad is angry or else.*
- *You could have done that better.*
- *People are jerks.*
- *You are a man, act like one.*
- *Accidents can lead to explosive moments.*
- *I taught you better than that!*

We all have our own list. Whether you realize it right now or not, you too have your own list of beliefs that comes from others. My mind accepted this information, as well as many other thoughts, concepts, and perceptions about life, as truth. Yet, wow. God is going to send me to hell for thinking of a girl's body part? **Really?** I was condemned by the age of twelve!

Looking at my list today, it is no wonder why I spent so many years in and out of self-judgment, distrusting myself and others, lacking confidence and clarity, and being fearful of living in my own skin.

Without knowing, it is with others' belief systems influencing us that we set out on our journey of life. Without a true understanding of who **we** really are, we begin to create someone else's idea of life! This is where most of us start! Mom and Dad, teachers, friends, a religious belief system, and something we took in from the evening news all tell us what to believe. Without a clue as to our own power, how to use this power, who or what we really are or what we deeply desire, we move about this life without the understanding that — through what we believe, think and speak — we are creating and molding our experiences.

Let me say that again:
THROUGH WHAT WE
BELIEVE,
THINK
& SPEAK
we are creating and molding
OUR EXPERIENCES.

Look back on your own life. What did you learn as a child, a teen or young adult?

- *Much of what is said to and about us when we are children is NOT true. Bringing awareness and processing these non-truths can free you up to live a life of fulfillment and possibility.*

- *We are molded and programmed by what we're immersed in as children, and this programming can absolutely be reversed or eliminated.*

- *Beliefs like "Life is hard" are absorbed from our environment and can operate under the radar of our consciousness, subtly keeping us from living our best life.*

- *We are far more powerful than we realize in terms of creating our own life circumstances. Realizing this provides opportunities to change our timeline and set us on a new path to a life of passion and excitement.*

See Workbook for
Activities and Exercises

CHAPTER TAKEAWAYS

{ CHAPTER 4 }

***

BUILD IT &
IT WILL COME

*How did I get **where I am today?***

It started in childhood. I recognized my parents' struggle. I saw the world through their eyes, through the eyes of my friends and through the neighborhood I grew up in. My mind identified with their struggle to get ahead, their lack of money and their lack of success — they didn't seem very happy. I said to myself I was not going to live this way.

What my Ego identified and heard was that money was the key to living life successfully. I heard it from society, from the media, from pop culture, from my friends, and from my parents. It became my goal: to be a man, to have a great income, to get a great job, to be able to support my loved ones, to have a nice home, with land, trees and fresh air. I built it. It came. The American way. A dream life.

Fiction, fiction, fiction!

That's what I discovered. The prescribed American Dream is pure fiction. Real happiness has nothing to do with your income or status.

There was one problem early on. I did not have the money to go to college, gain an education or learn a trade or skill. No one in my family had ever gone to college. There were obstacles to achieving an education, yet it was ingrained in me that this was the way to success. Receiving loans and grants still wasn't enough to pay the tuition and costs, so I joined the military to learn a skill and receive the VA benefit to assist me in paying my college tuition.

I was very focused on my dream. I was going to live differently than my parents. I did well in the military, becoming a Section Chief in two years, which is basically unheard of. My Dad had been the shining example of who to be and how to act in the Military.

After completing my tour of duty overseas, I applied and was accepted at Embry Riddle Aeronautical University. By this time, I was married. My wife and I struggled through my college days to make ends meet. The complaints I heard throughout my childhood — of never having enough money, food or love — haunted me. As the last semester approached, I was completely out of cash and my wife moved back home with her parents. I slept in my car for the last month of college, ate inordinate amounts of peanut butter and took showers at the pool. Nothing was going to stop me from my dream! I was determined. I was going to break free and be a real success.

The day came when I graduated with honors, and a few months later received my first job offer from a major international airline. I was on my way to all I dreamed of: a good income, a great career, a way to support my family, and the success I had so desired.

Or so I thought!

When I received my first paycheck, it would seem I had finally hit the jackpot. But today, I realize how even in the very beginning I felt disconnected and struggled to be there. In hindsight, it was obvious that this career path wasn't for me, but the lure of a big paycheck and the glory of this new found life stifled any hesitation.

I was late arriving for my first day of work and the excuses were plentiful — moving to another state, mishaps, traffic, not feeling well, etc. But, the bottom line - after all that hard work, I was not throwing away this career that would change my life. Not understanding my own belief system, I believed this was my first chance at leaving my struggles behind me. And thinking my discontent was temporary, onward I went. I showed up on time the very next day, and embarked on a long, "successful" career with the airline.

And yet, deep inside, **something stirred.**

I wondered what was wrong? Why was I not satisfied? I had put a lot of time and effort into forming this career. I can still hear my Ego mind taunting me:

- *"What, you don't like this?"*
- *"How could this be?"*
- *"You have worked so hard to get here!"*
- *"No, you don't like this. You can do better."*
- But, *"You have to like this because you will look like a fool if you leave!"*
- *"What will your friends and family think?"*
- *"This is the road to money, the house, the car and a successful life beyond beans and weinies!"*

This was my mind at work, injecting confusion, discouragement and ultimately discontent.

And I carried on.

I bought a big beautiful house on three wooded acres of land, complete with not one but two garages, an in-ground swimming pool, diving board and a 400-foot driveway. My friends all said, "Wow, look at you! How fantastic! All your hard work paid off, Mike!"

How cool is that? I had all the outward signs of success and the respect of my peers. I worked for the big company. I worked and I worked, crazy hours, sleeping at all hours during the day, going through the motions to accumulate more money, more status. I pushed aside what my heart was attempting to tell me. The voice of my heart began as a whisper, then a clear voice, until eventually it was booming inside me.

Yet the battle for supremacy continued for years: The Ego or the Heart, the Ego or the Heart. What my heart truly desired did not matter to the intellectual Ego.

Our Essence or Heart can be called the Divine or the Soul, the core being of each of us and our connection to God. God has also been called Source, Divine or the Universe. These are just words. Our Essence is the real us, the God in us and the voice of wisdom and higher truth. Yet, we so often can't hear our Essence over the obnoxiously loud and fearful voice of the Ego.

I let my intellect call the shots because it was all I knew. I identified with this life and this way of living. The great job, a great wife and a great house became a huge part of my identity. In fact, it *was* my identity. I had learned very well how to live from my Ego — what my mind believed I was and I identified with.

Though I didn't realize it at the time, I also was beginning to follow patterns of thinking and feeling I learned as a child. The concepts, perceptions, the things, people, the job, the house, my income, all solidly built an Ego identity — what my mind identified with and what I have now learned to address as the "Separate Self." The Separate Self Ego believes in separation, and being separate from others as well as separate from our Divine Essence.

*As I learned, and **you** will too,*
THIS IS *NOT* THE CASE.

My growing Identity continued to add to the list of identifiers of who I was:

- *Sgt. Michael Vukelic honorably discharged from the military.*
- *Top 7% Graduate of Embry Riddle Aeronautical University.*
- *A man with a big house, swimming pool, land and trees.*
- *The man paying big mortgage payments.*
- *Married to a High School sweetheart.*
- *A holder of an Airframe & Powerplant license.*
- *Strong.*
- *Successful.*
- *Intelligent.*
- *Handsome.*
- *Works for a major international airline.*
- *All of this and only 26 years old!*

Quite the epitome of success to my Ego mind!

Yet, the Ego still held on to the old beliefs that were very much a part of me:

- *You must work hard to be successful.*
- *Watch what you do because what will the neighbors think!*
- *You did not do that right.*

- *God is angry when we sin and we will go to hell for our sins.*
- *Stop crying or I will give you something to cry about.*
- *Love doesn't work very well.*
- *Make lots of money and you won't have to live like this.*
- *Life is hard.*
- *People are mean.*
- *God is always watching us and will punish you if you do something wrong.*
- *You could have done that better.*
- *People are jerks.*
- *You are a man, act like one.*
- *Accidents can lead to explosive moments.*
- *I taught you better than that!*

* * *

I BUILT IT – IT CAME: MY EGO STORY

*I was highly skilled at ignoring the **inner battle.***

My logical mind assured me that the Ego had made me successful in the military and it would make me successful now. I was flying high! Look at the man! I worked for the impressive company, made huge amounts of money, was married to the pretty wife, and was living in a beautiful house with all of the expensive toys. I had it all and I identified with it. I valued all that I had been taught to value. I laughed about it, looked down my nose at others, flaunted my success… and covered up my scars.

There were many great moments, I traveled, and my bank account grew. But all I manifested was coming from an egotistical value system. All the success came from the Ego identity, the smallest part of me. I was not really happy and my heart wanted to be somewhere else. I hoped that no one would see the battle that was taking place inside.

And then it happened. Slowly my life began to unravel. My marriage, my home and my life were falling apart. But my mind, convinced this is how I became successful and who I needed to be now began to point fingers and blame everyone else for my hardships and problems. I still identified with the man I had become — the rock solid man who had built his dream. The horror of not knowing what I would do if I sought change and *unidentified* with this life was paralyzing. I was a victim of my own thoughts.

Being in conflict with what I had learned as truth and had termed a "successful" life caused much confusion and inner turmoil. I had what I focused on and took action to achieve, yet I was nowhere near happy or *emotionally* successful. I was trapped by an attachment to my belief system and I would not let go. As much as I wanted to change my life, my fear still ruled my thoughts.

And besides, what would it look like if I left? The thought of "Look at all the money you are making!" overruled my heart and my deep desire to be free, fulfilled and live differently. I did my best to put on a happy face and keep playing the game of life under the Ego's rules, but inside the resentment and discouragement grew. I was at war with myself.

So, I did what I thought any self-respecting man would do. I worked even harder to pay those bills.

Working nights, my social life became nonexistent, as well as my quality relationships with others. Gradually, my wife and my friends drifted away as I became more irritated and discouraged. I told myself I didn't care. I told myself it was the job, it was the hours, it was anything but me. As my relationship with my wife ended, I found myself isolated and alone. My ego was now morphing into some sort of an angry, resentful identity that people distanced themselves from. Then, the news came.

*I found out I now had **cancer.***

Even though I believed that my life would be different than my parents if I had money, it was not! I had lots of money, but I didn't love my job, my house was a huge mortgage payment, I lost my wife, and now I had become diseased.

How could this be? I had worked hard, I excelled at school, in the military, at work. How could happiness elude me? Why do I feel so unfulfilled?

This was my journey — a huge life learning that would change me forever.

*At long last, the **pain became too much.***

Years of underlying unhealthy emotional states had taken their toll. Life seemed to be full of ugliness. I could not see my way out and at this time, I had no idea I was responsible for this mess called my life. I hid the discouragement and discontent from most people and sometimes I even convinced myself. I did not see that my thoughts of resentment, discouragement and the overall suffering were very much what I witnessed and experienced in my parents when I was a child. From an early age I had become accustomed to thinking and feeling in ways that were not healthy, and as much as I wanted to live differently, in many ways, I had become a mirror of my parents. And unconsciously, I was re-affirming my predominant feelings through my everyday experiences. A few short years later I would be shown it was time to wake up, time to become aware and re-assess my life.

***

BUILT IT,
BUT IT'S A *SHIT SHOW!*

By all respects my life should have been perfect. I was disciplined. I cared. I showed up. I worked hard. I maintained my list and checked it twice. I did all I believed I must do to be successful! And yet, here I was — alone, sick, and wallowing in victimhood.

*Little did I know, I was about to **hit rock bottom.***

One grey, windy January Chicago morning, I was driving home to my beautiful house in the country after working all night. It was my "Wednesday" — better known as "Sunday" to the rest of the world. I was excited — which was rare — to be heading home. It was cold and I was dead tired.

The thermometer read -9 degrees. My only desire was to get home and crawl into my warm bed. As I drove down the expressway, the car began to overheat and make strange noises. I thought, *"What?! More crap?!"* Without warning, the water pump failed. In that moment, my car seemed to be reflecting my discontent and wanted to give up and die on the side of the road.

Being the 90"s, this was prior to the boom of cell phones. I knew if I hesitated, there was a very real threat of freezing to death. To compound the situation, it was 7:15 on Sunday, there were very few cars on the road and in that cold, I didn't think anyone would stop to assist me! Somewhere between completely disgusted, thoroughly exhausted, and totally fed up, I decided to start the car back up and keep driving. My exit was fifteen miles down the road. As I drove, small wisps of smoke and disturbing wheezing sounds came from under the hood.

The engine stalled as I got close to my exit. I quickly discarded any ideas of walking to the nearest gas station or flagging someone down. I said to myself, *"Start the car again and keep going! Get yourself home!"* I made several attempts to start the car. I was conflicted as some part of me said, *"Stop! You are killing your car!"* Another part said, *"Who cares! You're killing yourself!"* I started the car and kept chugging on. Exhausted and half asleep, the cold kept me awake.

Then the *engine died* again.

I was a mile from home and without heat, frozen to my core. It was too cold to walk. After several attempts, somehow the car started. I had to push the gas pedal all the way to the floor to keep the car moving. Billowing smoke, bucking and backfiring, I kept going.

The scene was surreal. I lived in a beautiful area with the river, the trees, the country setting. As I drove, I tuned it all out. All I could think of was getting myself home and I did my best to ignore the horrible noises coming from the car. About fifty feet from my driveway, my "winter car" finally gave up with one loud bang. Surrounded by plumes of nauseating smoke, I resembled a miniature mobile forest fire. I lowered the driver's window to see my path as I coast on toward the apron of my driveway. At last, I had made it.

My car released a final hissing breath, and then... silence. For the first time in a very long time, I experienced utter silence. The car was now silent. My thoughts were silent. The early morning air surrounding my beautiful house - silent.

I was in full surrender and thoughtless. There was nothing left to think. All that remained in that moment was a feeling of pure exhaustion. And cold. Really cold.

Oh, I realized I had just trashed my car, but it no longer mattered.

My mind began to question:

WHAT JUST
HAPPENED?
Could this really be me?
THIS ISN'T ME;
Mike is
PERFECT
& HAS IT
ALL TOGETHER.

I had enough of my incessant mind, my intellectual Ego, and stopped my thoughts cold. I didn't know how I would get to work the next day, or whether I really wanted to.

*The answer was clear: **I didn't want to.***

I knew in that moment everything needed to change. This is what my successful life had come to. I was sick and struck with disease. I was disillusioned, discouraged and depressed. I was alone. I was angry. Minus the fact that I had some money — and the big bills that went along with it — I had become my parents. The patterns of behavior and thought with which they went through life had become a part of me.

I thought about my life, where I was, where I came from, and I dropped to my knees to pray. I asked for my life to change, to find my way back to joy. I prayed for friends, for laughter and for a return to health.

For the first time in a long time, I found myself curious again and a desire to know more was building within me. The questions came. *Am I throwing away the life I built? Am I really going to do this?* The fear was huge. The Ego hates to lose an identity. But, the answer was yes, it's finally time to change.

New questions came: *How do I build something else? What do I do first? Is there someone who can help me?*

I asked for a teacher to teach me what I need to know, to help me change my life. It was 7:45 am on a grey dreary day in January. Choking back tears of deep, profound pain, I listened to the wind howl outside as I drifted off to sleep.

- *The prescribed American Dream is pure fiction. Real happiness has nothing to do with your income or status.*

- *The Essence or Heart is the Divine or the Soul, the core of each of us and our connection to God, (Source, or Universe.) The Essence is the real us, the voice of wisdom and Higher Truth.*

- *The Separate Self — appropriately named the Ego — believes in separation, in being separate from others and from our Divine Essence.*

- *Confusion and inner turmoil often result from being in conflict with what you've learned from others as truth and what you feel and know in your Heart as a higher truth.*

- *When you find yourself in despair, a critical first step is to ask the right questions – such as How do I build something new and Who can help me?*

⇩

See Workbook for
Activities and Exercises

{ CHAPTER 5 }

***

The
DISCOVERY:
WE ARE NOT
Who We
BELIEVE
We Are

Through a cycle of getting curious, asking, and getting curious and asking once more, I began to discover life-changing knowledge. I experienced growth, self-discovery, self-empowerment and many amazing skillsets.

I began again.

When hearing these concepts for the first time from my teachers, I would always question their validity. Through many years of testing and experiencing the wisdom, I began to integrate the knowledge as truth.

I created a new path to an absolute truth. **You can too.**

***

A MOST IMPORTANT MIND-BLOWING TRUTH:

*Our life experiences are directly related to **what we think, feel and believe.***

Have you heard this before? It can be tough to swallow. I battled with this for years. *This can't be true,* I thought. Naturally, there are things in my life I do not like or experiences I don't enjoy. If I don't enjoy them and they don't make me happy why do I experience them? How could I be responsible for bringing them into my life?

We must begin with becoming aware — acutely aware — of what we have learned, where we place our focus each day, and what we think and feel about our work, our life, and the people we interact with.

The mind is the focusing mechanism in this world, and as you will see, your focus has a direct effect on your reality, your health, and the events, situations and experiences of your life. Many successful people — scientists, physicists, spiritual masters and teachers — understand this. I understand this now. It took a few years to incorporate this information fully into my life and at times my mind continues to challenge me, as the mind will always pick and choose what experiences it decides to own and what experience it believes someone else has caused. There was a time in my life when I would never have believed I created the uncomfortable situations and or ugly events in my life, but through great seeking, asking and experiencing, I have come to know this as truth.

At that time in my life, I assumed life happened to me. The world is already there and I am but a victim. Many of us believe this as this is what we are taught. We all must come to grips with our Ego mind. That baggage carrying identity we believe in does not have to be the boss. It's a process to move up the ladder of consciousness. And the lowest form of consciousness is victimhood.

* * *

ANOTHER MIND-BLOWING TRUTH:

*You are a **vibrational being of energy**.*

All of the brilliant scientists and spiritual masters who I have learned from absolutely believe we are affecting our own reality. It can be no other way in this three-dimensional world. What you say to yourself (your self-talk) what you say aloud and your thoughts about experiences, form your beliefs, create your emotional state and affect your life experience. A feeling is caused by a thought and simply put, the States of Mind or feelings that are created from your thoughts have an energy and a frequency. Each thought and the resultant feeling and reaction from the thought will change the energy of the body / mind. As the mind becomes focused in a thought, this energy change begins in the brain, where a chemical reaction occurs from each state of mind. As an example, with each thought causing anxiety, anger, sadness, grief or pain, we experience an emotion and an associated brain chemistry, which becomes stronger over time. Throughout life we are given opportunities through people, places and events to re-affirm our own predominant emotions.

The world will continually show us situations throughout life to reveal and re-affirm our own beliefs, behavioral patterning and predominant feelings. If you are not happy with what you see in your life, look no further than yourself for the solution.

BOOM!

From my earliest trainings and certifications, I learned how important it is to understand and grasp the science of the mind. Contrary to popular belief, it is not your heart that creates your feelings. Feelings actually originate in the Mind from thought, or patterns of belief and thought, that create a known and familiar chemistry. Each thought, combined with this chemistry can create powerful feelings. These feelings are then embodied by the body/mind and effect our overall energy.

Why is this so important? In philosophical terms, it is your feelings that the Universe, or God, responds to. Using scientific terminology, physics dictates that our thoughts and states of mind, (feelings) interact with The Quantum collective energy field that is always present.

*　*　*

A BIT OF SCIENCE

Most thoughts connect us to the past or a familiar and predictable future.

Each day as we awake our focus is on what we must do, who we will see, where we need to go and all the objects we own. Our attention is on what we must accomplish in a known and familiar reality. As we place our attention on these items we experience an associated emotion. Most emotions we feel are connected with memories of people, events or places at different times in our life. As we associate the emotion with something or someone in our life, we activate select neural pathways in the mind, connecting our present thought to relevant events from the past.

The result?

Much of our day, throughout many of our experiences, we are not 100 percent in the present moment. And we are influenced, or react to a conditioning from the events of our past. Further, each day as we continue to focus our attention on what is familiar and predictable, we have less and less attention or focus on creating anything new in our life. Thus, day in and day out, our life pretty much remains the same.

*We become **addicted** to our thoughts.*

Science backs this up. Your brain is a very sophisticated pharmacy. For every thought you have, and the feeling that follows, the hypothalamus assembles neuropeptides. These neuropeptides flood your bloodstream and then dock on receptors present on each cell in your body. That's a huge statement. You have approximately — by latest estimates — 37 trillion cells in your body. For every single thought you have, you create a State of Mind that creates this chemical reaction. There are different neuropeptides for grief, for anger, for anxiety, for lust, for happiness, for love, and your nervous system becomes continually more attuned to the associated chemical reaction within the body. As your cells divide and reproduce, they too have become more attuned to your predominant and repeated feelings and the resultant neuropeptides. If you repeatedly experience irritation, over time the receptors on each cell in your body will reproduce with more receptors for irritation and less receptors for other States of Mind, minerals and nutrients. As you become irritated on a regular basis, you are, in effect, becoming addicted to irritation.

The good news is, with discipline and the right tools, we can create new neural pathways and change our thoughts and feelings!

The mind has great power over you and your life. Every thought, your entire *belief system*, every *state of mind*, every *concept*, every *perception*, every *action*, every *reaction*, becomes your limited idea of self and what your mind identifies with. This becomes your Ego, or Separate Self identity. From this identity and the associated States of Mind, you experience and manifest your world.

This is my mind identity, my "Separate Self," the mind-created identity:

- *I am a white male.*
- *I live in Minnesota.*
- *I am 6 feet tall.*
- *I worked for a Big Corporation for 19 years.*
- *I have a pattern of expecting something strange to follow something good.*
- *I am a Life and Wellness Coach, Hypnotist and Inspirational speaker.*
- *I am the son of "Sally" and "Daniel."*
- *I am Divorced.*
- *I am 60 years old.*
- *I have a mind that likes to intellectualize and analyze.*
- *I have grey hair.*
- *I worked in Real Estate.*
- *I have money in the bank.*
- *I weigh 200 pounds.*

These are all things my mind identifies with. My identity. My mind also identifies with, and becomes addicted to, my recurring emotional states. Your mind, your Ego does the same for you.

This is not the
REAL YOU.

This is the
EGO-MIND
YOU.

- *Our life experiences are directly related to and effected by what we feel and believe to be true.*

- *Your mind is your focusing mechanism in this world. Your focus has a direct effect on your reality, your health, and the events, situations and experiences of your life.*

- *Your mind will always pick and choose what experiences it decides to own and what experience it believes someone else has caused.*

- *As we are conditioned as children to think and feel as our environment dictates, we become addicted to our predominant way we perceive and feel.*

- *You are a vibrational being of energy. The Universe, Source, Divine Essence, God... respond to your feelings and the energy you hold.*

See Workbook for
Activities and Exercises

{ CHAPTER 6 }

* * *

SEEKING
&
ASKING

Out of my seeking and asking, I was given more information. It was a process. A process of *unlearning* what I had learned since birth.

How had I become so out of touch with friends, with joy, and with life? I asked for truth. I prayed for knowledge. I prayed for a teacher that would teach me what I needed to know. I continued my search. The teachers came. They came beautifully and in perfect timing. Slowly my life began to change. My first teacher was Esther Hicks. She has written many books and Esther continues to present workshops regarding tapping into Infinite Intelligence.

When it was explained to me that there are three laws that govern our experience, The Law of Attraction, The Law of Deliberate Creation, and The Law of Allowing, life began to make some sense.

*The following are **brief descriptions** of these 3 laws:*

LAW OF ATTRACTION

The Law of Attraction is the attractive, (magnetic) power of the Universe that draws similar energies together. It manifests through the power of creation, everywhere and in many ways. The law attracts thoughts, ideas, people, situations and circumstances that hold similar energy or vibration.

LAW OF DELIBERATE CREATION

The Law of Deliberate Creation is the act of deliberate focus on our desires. Getting clear on our inner most desires, writing them, speaking them with feeling and authority and using the Law of Attraction to bring these desires into our life.

LAW OF ALLOWING

The Law of Allowing states that once we are clear on our dreams and desires and we focus on deliberately manifesting those dreams and desires, through thought, visualization or the written word, we can enhance the effectiveness of the Law of Attraction by believing in the process and allowing those dreams to come true without our usual doubt or fear. We "know" that through clarity, focus, and belief and the positive emotions that follow our thought, we can, "allow and trust" our dream to become our reality.

In learning these laws, I started to change my thinking. I began to shift my focus to what I wanted and I wrote about it each day. Mysteriously what I focused on would show up. I learned that it is not so mysterious after all – it is the way the world works!

I continued to ask and be curious. I learned how to live from my Divine Essence (my Heart) and stop listening to the chattering mind. I was integrating information not just on an intellectual level, but learning to understand new wisdom and embody this into my life. A shift was taking place. A sparkle returned to my eye.

Then my life faltered. My intellectual self (my Ego mind) would take over again. I had left my job, my wife was gone, I was rebuilding and not making much money. My Ego would return along with the old belief systems and my old list. I would fall back to my pattern of resentful, upset and discouraged thinking because I had become addicted to the way it made me feel. My mind would tell me that I should feel awful. Just as I learned in childhood, I was hard on myself. I would wallow in self-judgment. In my old way of *feeling* about life, I would return to the role of the victim. I was wrestling with an old identity and a known belief system.

Yet part of my new learning was starting to take hold. It was a process, a process for growth. I asked for more teachers. I worked with healers, Hypnotherapists, Reiki, and energy healers. I trained with Mike Dooley, an author of several successful books, a speaker and trainer, and is most known for his "Notes From the Universe." I was offered a spot to train with Jack Canfield, also a successful author and trainer, most notably known as the co-creator of *Chicken Soup for the Soul* series. Jack offers a one-year "Train the Trainer" program for his "Success Principles."

My life was improving, but my addictive thoughts and beliefs wreaked havoc with my life. I would feel awful. Then I would feel great. Then I would return to feeling discontent, discouraged, and depressed. I grew up with discipline and perfection in the house and it was difficult to be "good enough." My Ego identity was alive and well and still had me in its grip. It was relentless. I was up and down and then I would invite myself back into the process of healing. My growing awareness would not let me sink back down to the depths of despair for good.

But I questioned myself. I had done a lot of training and personal growth work. I now knew The Secret, the book and movie released in 2002 regarding instruction on how to create your desires. So why was I not "super successful"?

My unconscious mind would run the old program: "This is who you are. I know you! You are not doing this right! You are a resentful, discouraged person!" Consciously, I would tell myself I was valuable, knowledgeable, intelligent, but the world in front of me showed me "my truth." I was not making much money and not contributing to the world. Then I would dive back into what I had recently learned. Positive thinking and visualization would work and things would pick up. Then life would shift and fall apart. Back and forth, back and forth, I would sabotage my own success with my old ingrained belief system. What a vicious cycle!

Then I joined Jack's "Train the Trainer" program of self-empowerment. I loved it yet I also felt out of my comfort zone. It felt good to be around other people after so many years of working the night shift and feeling alone. I thought this new life was great and then again it was terrifying. I worked closely with several of the participants in the program. We did all types of exercises, speaking in groups and began the process of releasing our fears and defining our future. I thought I was doing so well!

One day a fellow trainer offered up a deck of healing cards and asked me to pick a card. Of course! Sure, I can't wait to hear what the Universe has to say to me! I pulled a card that read: "Let the healing begin!" I was dumbfounded. Let the healing begin? I felt as though the healing was over. I had done a lot of inner work and felt great — or so I thought. I put the card back in the deck and she offered to reshuffle. I pulled another card. Guess what? Holy shit, I pulled the same card! "Let the healing begin!" Little did I know that yes, I was just beginning.

***

LEARN TO UNLEARN

Why was the self-empowerment training uncomfortable? Consciously, I was still very aware of recent events, and in my new life experience, my ego was feeling not good enough, and so out of its usual comfort zone. As I worked on and became aware of my limited concepts, and self judgments, I uncovered beliefs and childhood events that had shaped my perceptions and ideas of life. As a child, without any real understanding I had experienced traumatic physical and emotional events that my mind was unable to make sense of. Unconsciously, I carried baggage from these events which caused resentment and a lack of love for self.

I would consciously say, "Look at me. I'm courageous, I have done well in the military, smart, graduated college with honors, and successful, I landed my big-time job." But unconsciously I was repeating an old story. Every time success came, whether it was a relationship, a new pursuit, a career or a moneymaking opportunity, I was blindsided by something ugly. It didn't make sense, but there it was every time!

I believed and identified with a person who thought money made him valuable, felt alienated and "separate" and did not see a lot of "good" in life. Although I could not see it, I was hard on myself, and my thoughts held a lot of negativity, judgment and resentment. And since I saw this in the world - it was a part of me. I struggled to achieve a great life.

As a child I felt the feelings of happiness as well as pain and hurt. Up until this point in life each day was a roller coaster experience of positive and negative emotion. As my mind/body sought to feel and re-affirm my addictive predominant feelings, many exciting and many uncomfortable and life-altering situations would present themselves. One day, I might receive a raise at work and take off on a 3 day vacation, and the next day, despite being an excellent employee, the airline would decide to downsize and I was targeted with paperwork that stated "you must immediately relocate or resign." Just as I learned in childhood, when things were going well I should expect something ugly was lurking. Having learned at an early age the feelings of hurt, and pain went along with happiness, many situations confirmed a belief that life is hard, and people are mean. The downsizing was a prime example of how the company management team gave me the opportunity to re-affirm my own addictions to pain, hurt and victimhood. It would be a few years before I learned to break free of this cycle.

Continuing my quest for success, I trained with a fantastic mentor, started a real estate business and made investments in several properties. I did very well with these investments. Yes, the driven Mike was a huge success and could do anything he put his mind to and create abundance. And then I found myself in the 2008 to 2011 real estate market collapse. I made a great deal of money in real estate, but wham — something awful would always come along and sabotage my joy. It was relentless. It was exhausting! And even though I was not aware of it, it was just as I believed.

Love and relationships? I had great relationships over the years, and they would play out just as I believed. The playful beginning was an adventure and that was a blast, but just as I witnessed in childhood, "love didn't work very well." Sooner or later every one of them would end. Even the very best and most loving relationship would falter. I did not understand either parties "Separate Self" patterns and beliefs and rather than learning and growing the "we" I would choose to remain autonomous and end the relationship before it had a chance to cause pain. I feared the pain. I resisted the pain. Therefore I recreated it again and again in my life. As soon as the relationship became the slightest bit difficult I (the Ego) would decide I was not getting my needs met and it was over. It was discouraging, but better than a lifetime of pain. Over many years and experiences, I've found that knowing and understanding our Separate Self is huge to understanding each other and embracing a healthy, happy relationship.

It was just as my mind believed:

Life is hard.
PEOPLE ARE JERKS.
LOVE DOESN'T
WORK VERY WELL.
Money is the only thing of value.

These unconscious beliefs caused a lot of grief in my life. I re-affirmed the emotions and proved myself right again and again. And it was showing up in many ways.

Through attending the intense Canfield Train-the-Trainer course, I learned the Success Principles and how to process triggers. Triggers are what happens when the Ego reacts to situations, events, people and conversations that cause negative emotions. When we are triggered, we are reacting to something the Ego mind believes to be real.

If I told you, "I think your green hair is ugly" and you know that you don't have green hair, it will not bother you. If I said, "I think you are fat and ugly", if any part of your Ego believes this, you will trigger and react with anger or hurt. This is your Ego.

I learned how to focus on my desires. Things would improve, but the roller coaster life still presented itself. At times, I still played a victim of circumstance, blaming and pointing the finger at people, situations and events.

But, I never gave up. I continued to ask and be curious, as I was not going to settle for a roller coaster life or be willing to sit on the sidelines. Just as I had done in the past, I asked for my next teacher and this one would be a doozy.

The Universe provided my next teacher in the form of an Enlightened Master. The beautiful wisdom I received from this sage finally reached my hardened heart and changed my life forever. This knowledge would identify and create awareness of my belief system and my patterning. I gained a valuable education of science and spiritually and empowered myself to understand what life is all about. Over the next four years, I learned a great deal of information and began to integrate and embody the knowledge. Finally!

I discovered what to embrace and what to drop. I began to Self-Realize (self-realization is a true understanding of our Authentic or True Essence) and understand the difference between who I was raised to believe I was and who I really am. Most importantly, I began to understand what held me back from living the life I've always imagined and how to embrace life's magic!

It was all me:

- *My Patterns.*
- *My Thoughts.*
- *My Belief System.*
- *My Emotions.*
- *My Ego.*

I learned to become aware of, all that my mind had come to know as truth! I was, for the first time in my life, truly happy, at peace and fulfilled! The transformation was amazing.

This information was the key to finding my freedom and my joy!

And now
I WISH
to
SHARE IT
WITH YOU!

- *There are three laws that govern our experience — The Law of Attraction, The Law of Deliberate Creation, and The Law of Allowing.*

- *You can learn to live from your Divine Essence (your Heart) and stop listening to the chattering Ego mind, by integrating information not just on an intellectual level, but embodying the wisdom into your life.*

- *While you're on your journey of greater self-awareness, many opportunities will present themselves in an attempt to re-affirm your addictive predominant feelings.*

- *Triggers are what happens when the Ego Identity reacts to situations, events, people and conversations that cause negative emotions. When we are triggered, we are reacting to something the Ego mind believes to be real.*

- *Self-realization is an optimum state of understanding our Authentic Self or Essence vs. who we have been conditioned to believe we are. It is an understanding of the difference between what we have been taught to believe and the magnificence of the true self.*

⇩

See Workbook for
Activities and Exercises

* * *

CHAPTER 7

The
BASICS:
SCIENCE &
SPIRITUALITY

Bridging the Thinking (Ego) Mind, (the intellectual processing of knowledge created by our environment and societal input) and the Knowing (Divine) Mind (Our connection to Infinite intelligence and wisdom from our true Divine Essence) is perhaps a balancing act, but with awareness and focus the Divine mind can become integrated and a rewarding new experience.

*Let's begin with **Science vs. Spirituality.***

Many of us believe Science and Spirituality are very different. Through years of study, I have uncovered the truth that Science and Spirituality are more alike than most of us think.

LET ME SHARE AN OVERVIEW TO ILLUSTRATE.

Science and Quantum Physics tell us:

1. At the most basic level, *we are all one.* Matter is made up of molecules. Molecules break down to Atoms. Atoms break down to energy. Lots of energy.

2. *Everything* in our three-dimensional world is energy. This includes you.

3. You are an *observer* or energy being having an experience in physical form.

4. Your *energy changes* with your thought and subsequent state of mind.

5. Your mind is the most *sophisticated pharmacy* in the world. You become familiar with, and addicted to, patterns of thought and emotional states.

6. You are affecting your reality (physical matter) constantly with focused thoughts. *Energy flows where your attention goes.* Thoughts from the mind are bits of information that redirect matter and form.

7. *As you focus the mind* on people, your pain, your job, your family, your partner, your body, your computer, the car, the kids, or Facebook, you are activating a known neurological network in your mind and collapsing *infinite possibilities* — into the same patterns — called your life!

8. If you use your boss to re-affirm your *addiction to not being worthy,* or the news to reaffirm your addiction to irritation, or a relationship to reaffirm your *addiction to suffering,* you are giving your power away to something or someone in your life.

9. The possibilities of life are infinite, and you are one of many possibilities.

Spirituality tells us:

1. The Father, the Son, the Spirit *are all one.* You are an expression of God, the creator.

2. God, Source, The Universe is Love and is *omniscient and omnipotent.* God is always with you, is everywhere and is therefore is inside you and a part of you.

3. Your mind — through thoughts, beliefs and your states of mind — can alter your experience and taint your perception of your reality.

4. You are "Divine Essence," a spiritual being or soul having an experience in physical form. You are not the being your Ego mind believes you are.

5. Through-out your physical experience, growth, and learning in life, you are expanding the universe as well as universal knowledge.

6. There is not a *"Good and Bad"* — it is just your "Separate Self" belief that labels your experience this way. All experiences are for uncovering and encompassing wisdom and ultimately *Love*. Everything is perfect in Gods world.

7. Life mirrors back to you through events, people and situations what you talk about, think about, and feel. In short, you reaffirm what you believe to be true.

8. The Ego is attached to an identity. What we do, what people think of us, what we have. If we lose one identity, it will quickly attach to another. The Ego does not care if our identity is identified with pain or not. It's an identity. A Separate Identity. Some Egos create a "pain body" and will create enough pain in one's life to awaken them beyond their Ego identity. Witness my rock-bottom moment in my driveway that cold, Chicago morning. The Ego is the so-called "Devil."

9. When you believe it, you will see it.

Some of us naturally have a scientific mind. As a technical person, I spent many years in my mind, intellectualizing, analyzing and overthinking everything. Some of us are more spiritual or heart centered. In any lifetime, we may be called to live from our heart and embrace our Essence. Just as many Masters have done, any one of us may experience enough suffering to awaken or become aware of the self serving Ego — and begin to live life from our heart. Our challenge is to be without judgment toward either belief system when choosing to learn about Spirituality or Science, without preference, without a right or wrong, without judgment toward yourself or others for the direction and journey of a chosen life. We are all learning or experiencing our growth in Divine perfection and Divine timing.

Life is not a race or a competition. You did not come to be better than or less than. You came to be happy in this experience. You came to expand, grow, be fulfilled and know Love. God, the Universe, your Essence, is Love.

I have been educated by many successful people and institutions and currently hold degrees in Technology, Business and Metaphysics. Not that this really matters. The most profound life-changing information came from a combination of Masters. The following concepts changed the way I understand myself, the world and my experiences, which ultimately facilitated a major breakthrough in my life.

These following concepts are a condensed version of the Quantum Leap process clients enjoy, as they learn to let go of a limiting and somewhat painful identity. Releasing old programming, beliefs and patterns, is life changing and is key to embrace a new healthy, happy, prosperous self. Through fun retreats and events many "successful" people learn new tools and ways to follow their inner guidance to heal their challenges. And while many earn a great income and have great careers, they have become increasingly aware that something is amiss from their experience and there must be more to life.

The uncovering of a "Separate Self Identity," creating awareness of "A Story" and understanding the mind's role in the events of our life, open the door to creating a life filled with miracles. As we live with this integrated knowledge and the awareness of our own power, there will be many massive shifts in relationships, career, and the peace and all-encompassing bliss from life.

This Divinely-inspired information has been accumulated over several years and are uncommon steps to freedom, peace and an "Outrageously Successful" life. As I stated, I didn't just wake up one day and get it. I had a back and forth pattern of starting to believe and then falling back into my old patterns. It is often the same for clients, but my "Quantum Leap System" of teaching has shortened the learning curve considerably! You do not have to take years to start living successfully and embody the miracle that is you!

Taking a Quantum Leap for life involves 3 major steps:

1. Understanding the Ego or Separate Self Identity
2. Love Thyself
3. The End Results

Combining 17 years of personal growth and development, I use these three amazing steps to create optimum peace, joy, freedom and empowered living. Each section includes wisdom from the realm of Science, Physics, New Age Spirituality and Psychological techniques. It is not a coincidence that you have this book in your hands, it is time for you to begin to integrate this wisdom.

- *Bridging the Thinking Mind (the intellectual processing of knowledge created by our environment and societal input) and the Knowing Mind (Our connection to Infinite intelligence and wisdom from our true Essence) is a balancing act, but Science and Spirituality are more alike than most of us think.*

- *Your mind is the most sophisticated pharmacy in the world. You become familiar with, and addicted to, patterns of thought and emotional states.*

- *The Ego does not care if our identity is identified with pain or not. It's an identity. Some Egos create a "pain body" and will create enough pain in one's life to awaken them beyond their Ego identity.*

- *You did not choose life to be better than or less than. You came to be happy in this experience. You came to expand, grow, be fulfilled and know Love. God, the Universe, your Essence is Love.*

- *Uncovering your Ego or "Separate Self Identity," creating awareness of "Your Story" and understanding the mind's role in the events of your life are critical to creating a life filled with miracles.*

See Workbook for
Activities and Exercises

* * *

CHAPTER 8

The
SEPARATE
SELF IDENTITY

The beliefs. The patterns. Your experiences. Your stories. All of these create a limited personal identity that you believe in and attach to. You have a story to tell, and you want us to believe you! It justifies who you are, what you have been through, what you have become and why you are not as successful or outgoing or abundant as you would like. You feel better when others can commiserate with your story. Sometimes, you hide behind a story hoping no one can see the real you. But the truth is, you can't hide. We are not separate. Everyone can see the real you. Most of us don't say anything to point out your challenges, but the people, conversations and events acting as mirrors of your deepest beliefs will do so and it upsets you. These (mirrors) can make you react. You react because the Separate Self believes what they say is true and you must defend who you are, what you have become, and your story!

Just as I have shared my patterns, my belief system based on my upbringing, and the further experiences of my life had me believing in my story, most of us have a story we tell ourselves. It is how the "Ego" mind works. With every client, this is where we begin, by breaking down their story.

I have worked with business people, entrepreneurs, professionals of all stripes, and the details might differ, but the gist is the same. Many of us have various levels of pain in our life that we will address, or live with. Is this pain absolutely necessary? No. The pain is an opportunity to become part of our growth. If you could change your thoughts, right now, — all you believe and the story you tell yourself, — your entire life would change! The problem is, many of us cannot or will not change what we believe and think. It is a conditioned aspect of us.

You might be a successful business person and by all standards appear to have it all. Yet something inside you feels unfulfilled, agitated, or alienated. It is a process to reveal your "Shit Show" and change. Many of us will defend our story until we are one day in a medical facility, wondering how did I get here?

Stories are powerful and
*create **emotional reactions.***

To be healthy, authentic and successful it's very powerful to release your old "Story."

As children we loved when Mom and Dad would tell us bedtime stories. As we got older, we loved the stories people would tell us that made us laugh or made us cry. The stories seemed innocent enough. There are stories in movies, stories in books, speaking events with a good story, and stories of love and joy and laughter as well as stories of challenge and triumph and success. We have learned to identify with a good story! Many of us have personal stories of joy and success or painful stories of heartbreak or failure. Everybody loves a good story!

We also have a personal story that's been ingrained in our minds. While some stories can be empowering and supportive for us, others can limit our success. Even though the original story may be just a memory, that story has become an integral part of our life and our identity and until we change the story, we may continue to experience the story for an entire lifetime. What the mind has come to believe is present in that story and we will continue to recreate that story in our life in many different ways, through events, situations and in our interaction with others. You may be familiar with the statements — "I just can't get a break!" or "Why do these things keep happening to me?" and the story that follows.

There are several factors that keep the story in play. Over time we become addicted to our emotional story. Just like any other addiction, it makes us feel something. As we know, every emotion we feel creates a chemical reaction in the mind and body. The rush of this chemistry is addicting. Thus, your thoughts and your story are addicting.

We may really believe that someone or something in our life has done us wrong. These events cause us to believe we are a victim. Through blaming and pointing the finger at the situation, the event or the person we create familiar similar emotions and an energetic bond to the emotion that is hard to break. The only way out of this victimhood, which I have learned through my spiritual teachings and by experience, is in understanding that the situation, person or event is there in your life to reveal wisdom, a belief, a concept or a story that hinders your growth.

The familiar thoughts and emotions reappear again and again in various ways to re-affirm and validate your story. For example, if you have it ingrained in you that your life has been hard, you will continue to see that play out in your life story. It's the same with "people cannot be trusted" or "love doesn't work very well". Your life will bring countless examples of this belief into your awareness, along with all the associated emotions.

The Separate Self loves a good story. Especially if the story makes you feel the way you have become accustomed to feeling, and reaffirms your known identity. The Ego does not care what the identity is as long as it has an identity. Even a negative identity will do.

Through out my life experiences, my old story would usually return to pain. Even the best experiences of my life would later become identified as a bummer. I was conditioned to think this way. No matter how long we have been repeating a story, it only takes a moment to change that story and our experience. Bringing my story into my awareness was powerful, enabling myself to take ownership and shift my focus from the known and familiar experiences and emotions tied to the past, which then allowed new, refreshing experiences, happiness and success into my life. Taking the wisdom from my story and leaving the story behind me, leaves the energy of the story in the past and now enables me to maintain a focus in the infinite present moment.

***

HOW YOUR EXPERIENCE BECOMES A REPEATED 3D REALITY

A two-year-old, just learning how to walk, is out jumping, playing and running through the grass. Loving the moment and so excited to be experiencing a beautiful day. Suddenly, he is violently grabbed from behind, picked up and thrown across the road, landing in the grass.

Immediately the child experiences the State of Mind of confusion, shock, disbelief, paralyzing fear and hurt. In an instant, the mind begins searching for answers: *Wow, what just happened? Why did this happen? This does not feel good. How did I get here?* The mind splinters in many directions attempting to understand and "make sense" of what happened in the midst of the physical and emotional pain.

The same child a few years later is playing a game of running bases with his friends. Standing there with his friends he is caught by surprise as he is violently grabbed from behind by the hair on his head, dragged into the house and thrown headfirst sprawling on the floor.

Again, the boy experiences hurt, confusion, shock, disbelief, and paralyzing fear. *What just happened? Why did this happen? Did I do something wrong? This person loves me, what did I do?* The mind is confused and can perceive the experience in many ways. Does this person love me? What is important here is what the mind decides to take in as truth. The boy, just having fun with friends, is jolted into an unpleasant experience and unconsciously believes he must have done something wrong. In this case the mind adopts a self-judgment and begins to form beliefs: *I didn't do something right or I would not be treated this way!* Feeling bad, the boy suffers. He is confused and angry. A fear based, Separate Self identity is being formed. It does not matter if it is true or not, it matters what the mind decides is true.

Later in life, the boy, who is now a young man, is overseas in the military, and out flying all day on maneuvers. He arrives back at the base to be told his wife is cheating on him. He again experiences the predominant states of mind of hurt, shock, confusion, disbelief and ultimately pain. Wow, why did this happen? The mind searches and finds something it can identify with: Did I do something wrong? Doubts appear. An opportunity arises to engage the Ego belief of not loved. This person loves me, why did this happen? The false belief system of "not enough," or "not doing something right" are becoming stronger. Again experiencing pain, the man is now becoming increasingly hurt and fearful. He asks himself, "Why is this happening," "What's next?", dreading the answer.

Still later in a corporate career, the man is blindsided and receives a shocking letter from the company, which is downsizing and moving people around, telling him to relocate or resign! Even though the event is a blessing in disguise and a perfect way to change his miserable experience there, the mind identifies with more shock, hurt, confusion, disbelief and finally pain.

Yet again he asks himself, *What is wrong here? Why is this happening to me? What did I do wrong? Is God punishing me?* Adding to his repetitive hurt and pain, the man does not feel valuable or loved. Wrestling with confusing thoughts and feeling victimized, he lashes out and tells himself its the company. These people are mean! The man, again in disbelief and shock, now adds anger to his experience and believes he must protect himself. He reacts toward the offender, pointing the finger at the company as the ultimate problem.

As the body mind seeks to experience the addictive thought and emotional states, the grown successful man, now investing in real estate, has yet another opportunity to experience shock, disbelief, hurt, confusion and anger as troublemakers in the neighborhood are continually damaging one of his properties. Having felt this way in the past, his body and mind react strongly, as he tells himself a repeated story of pain. *What is happening here? Why does this happen to me? Something is not right!*

What did I do to ***deserve this?***

Building more anger and resentment, he again identifies himself as a victim. Yes, the kids are mischievous and causing trouble and should be arrested. The larger and important point I want to make here is: *the man would not be in this situation if he did not have a recurring pattern of pain and suffering!* Doubting his path to success he finds himself in shock and anger. He is a victim of his own Ego mind.

Through feeling the similar emotions over many years, the man has become addicted to feeling pain. Since he was a young boy, each time he is feeling good, he is blindsided with a hurtful event. After several years, he has created a story. "Every time things are going well, something awful happens." He is not aware of his own repeated states of mind of confusion, disbelief, shock, and anger and has built a strong connection to many events which have become an identity - and not a very happy one at that. His Separate Self identifies with his experience and creates further events to re-affirm the suffering, the resentment and confusion again and again.

In order for the
EGO TO
SURVIVE,
it must have
AN IDENTITY.

As long as the man is not consciously aware of his pattern, the childhood conditioned thought and emotion rule his life. This identity survives only because he unconsciously identifies with it and continues to react to it. The man at this point is not feeling very valuable, loved, happy or successful and he can't explain why these events keep happening to him! His hurt, confusion, and suffering are something he has re-affirmed since childhood. His mind cannot see the pattern in his life or the recurring states of mind as the situations and events do not appear similar. Unable to effect the change he desires, he becomes discouraged and opens himself up to a hopeless, depressive state.

Until the initial childhood event was eventually disclosed by family, and a door opened to become aware of his own fearful thought and negative story, his pattern of pain continued. And his "Successful Discontent," with life, love and his career remained very real to him!

You likely recognize me as the man in the story, but do you also recognize a pattern in your life in any way?

***

HOW A SIMPLE "IDENTITY" IS FORMED

A young boy in elementary school does very well in Math. He is commended for his excellence and everyone praises him. He experiences joy, love, excitement and his Ego declares: "Wow, I am good at math!"

Progressing through school, the boy does well in English. He is commended for his excellence in English and everyone praises him for doing well. He experiences joy, love, excitement and receives high fives from his friends. His mind is now building a Separate identity: "Wow, I am a good student in English!

The same boy, believing and identifying with being a good student, does well in Science. He is commended for his excellence in Science and his teacher, friends and parents praise him. He experiences joy, love, excitement and high fives from his friends. His mind, pumping up his ego, is becoming attached to and has created an identity: "Wow, I am a really great student!"

The boy believes he is a great student. He is "better than" most students. This is his story. The Ego loves this and becomes attached to this story and now it is a part of his identity. He feels great! The boy enters college with the strong belief that he is a great student.

But he does poorly in his first year. Even though he may have picked an inappropriate subject or his heart is guiding him in a new direction, the Ego wreaks havoc with the boy as now he is immersed in an experience where his identity has been ravaged. *What is happening? Am I not a great student?* Self-doubt creeps in. He experiences States of Mind of hurt, pain and failure, as the Ego instantly searches for a new identity and attaches to a new story that doesn't feel good.

This is the human Ego mind. Living without an understanding of the Ego can cause great pain, or at a minimum, a roller coaster of negative and positive experiences. If the boy goes through life attached to what he believes he should be, rather than accepting his experience as perfection, he will create more pain. While it is important to receive praise and love your talents, successes and gifts, being unattached to the way your life progresses and loving the wisdom in your experience keeps the Ego identity from ruling our life.

***

LIVING FROM THE HEART

Living life from our heart or "Divine Essence" is living without the frustration of a repeating story. We are empowered. We understand the role of the story and our Separate identity. Supportive of a full life, we live each day with awareness, able to choose joy, without judgment of ourselves or our experience. We are free to embrace a new perspective - of life's inherent perfection. Living from our Divine Essence is a new way of "being" in the moment and having the experience of events and situations without connecting to a *past memory.*

*It may not seem like it at first, but this kind of living is **absolutely possible!***

Your Essence is the pure God within you. When you leave the physical realm, the physical body, you will return to your Essence. The Essence does not worry, knows how incredible and extraordinary you are and is with you every day! Being without the concept or attachment to "good" or "bad," your Essence is in a constant state of bliss! It does not identify with Separation. It has no fear and sees life as a perfect learning journey. Tapping into your Essence will create great peace in your life while you follow your joy and serve the world in ways you have yet to imagine.

The key to healing and loving our life experience is in the acceptance of our perfect journey and in the release of the thoughts, patterns and beliefs that limit our joy and love for ourselves.

BECOME AWARE OF THE STORY WE REPEAT TO OURSELVES.

*This is the first step to **living a free, fulfilling and successful life!***

Get curious and reflect on your life. What are your repeated life experiences? What story or stories do you tell yourself? Are you consciously aware of your stories or are they hidden? Is there a predominant State of Mind associated with your story? Let your mind focus on a particular subject now and be aware of how the mind connects with past experiences.

Your mind believes your story and makes it true! What do you identify with? Take a moment, a day or a week to become aware and write down your thoughts regarding your stories and recurring states of mind. This is how you learn the construct of your mind.

***

MIND BASED LIVING

Becoming aware of the mind and how it works is essential in changing how you perform through-out life, and how you feel.

The mind cannot be "fixed," but it can be rewired. What you believe you believe, what you are conditioned to think you think, and what you experience you come to expect. This builds a neural network in the brain that predetermines our model of the world and how we perceive people, our career, our level of abundance and our health. Through changing our thoughts, concepts, perceptions, and stories we rewire our neural network and our predominant way of perceiving ourself and our life.

Your mind only has the capability to see what its conditioned to see. For example, a camera recording of a particular scene will see more than the human mind looking at the same scene. Why? First, the human body sends 11 million bits of information to the brain every second. But, the brain can only process 50 bits per second. And number two, through our judgments, attachments, experiences and beliefs, the mind will perceive what is most important or familiar to our mind. In short, we are missing information in our environment all the time.

A great example of this is a story I was told some time ago. Most of us are familiar with the story of Christopher Columbus, the explorer that went down in history for his discovery of America. But are you familiar with another, very surprising and eye-opening portion of this story that states Mr. Columbus's ships were anchored offshore for many hours and unrecognized by the natives of the islands? The mind of the natives, never having seen anything of this nature or a ship of this size were not able to see Columbus's ships in the water. It took a native Shaman, who first noticed ripples on the water that were unfamiliar, to recognize something was different and finally see the ships to then convince the members of the tribe that there were indeed ships anchored off shore. Most of us have had this experience at one time or another at different times in our life and we are not aware of it.

The mind also creates and assimilates patterns of thought and behavior. The events, people, places, things and experiences of our life all have an association with one another in the mind. One thought and a subsequent feeling is connected to many past life events. The more we place thought on a person, place or thing and have a repetitive emotional reaction, the stronger the neural net in the mind becomes.

But it does not mean old thoughts will rule your life forever. Even though some neural pathways are deeply ingrained in our mind, we now know, through studies in neuroplasticity, that it is possible to create new neural pathways in the brain.

Through choosing new thoughts, and interupting the old ways of thinking, we can create new neural pathways and over time unwire an existing neural net in the brain. That is the amazing good news — we can create new neural pathways and disconnect the old associated neural net of events, people, and things, creating change and a new focus. The deeper wisdom here is to understand that the mind — through beliefs, concepts and perceptions — *will constantly see what it associates with and believes is true.*

We are habitual creatures. We each tend to focus in the same way each day. Some people, events and situations are very positive for us and create joy, and other negative situations are where we can learn the most valuable lessons. Through our own negative thought and focus, many of us give our power away to people and events outside of ourselves...

- *...if we use our boss* to re-affirm our addiction to judgement.

- *...if we use a co-worker* to re-affirm our addiction to irritation.

- *...if we use our relationship* to re-affirm our addiction to suffering.

- *...or if we use the news* to re-affirm our addiction to anger.

We are activating an established network in the mind and a related emotional response.

This response does two things:
- It connects us with our past as emotions are chemical residues associated with an event, person or place in the past.

- It also acts as a siphon, taking our energy and focus away from the present and into the past.

When this occurs we are giving our own power away to something or someone in our lives. The stronger the emotion becomes, the stronger the bond and the focus on the cause of it.

We have come to this physical experience, to life, to expand, to live in joy and to grow in knowledge and awareness. How we experience life is up to us.

Most likely, we have all heard the wisdom stating, "Just let it all go!" While it seems easy enough, from my professional experience once you have experienced repetitive trauma, its harder than most think to release it from our mind. The mind, as it attempts to keep us safe from further hurt, is in resistance to similar painful emotional experiences. In these situations, as long as the Ego (Separate Self) resists, we most likely will react and ultimately resist our own healing. Once we can stand back from our negative situation, become aware and accept the higher wisdom and understand, this is our place of vulnerability, we can stop blaming and pointing the finger, stop resisting and heal. The only way out of the ugliest situations in your life is to realize its coming from a pattern of your thoughts and your beliefs.

Pushing away or stuffing our feelings and blaming others will not heal and transform our life. In doing so, we allow the repetitive thought and emotional energy to remain with us and be re-experienced again and again. That's when life is beautiful and then gets ugly... rinse, repeat. We must stop identifying with and regurgitating the old concepts, beliefs and the "story" to free ourselves and miraculously change our experience of life.

Most of us operate as if today were yesterday and many of our interactions and experiences cause a familiar reaction. When we live in awareness in the present, focused on joy, choosing healthy thought, we are operating as an integrated whole and are no longer the body mind emotional person that is experiencing reaction after reaction.

Through out childhood and beyond, we perceive information from our family, our friends, and society that shape our thought. We are experiencing many old paradigms and daily situations that create a Separation from others.

Sitting in the classroom at school, we perceive everyone as separate from us. Sitting in church, we look to the crowd and see a room full of different people. Through out your life the mind believes that in being separate you are different and special, and will create all kinds of ways to prove this to us - including a separate identity, our own special challenges, and level of intelligence. This is the Separate Self, where comparison, pain and judgment are born. You are black, I am white, I have this special challenge, you don't, I do this work, I have this problem, therefore you are not like me.

Your highest truth, your Divine Essence, has zero judgment, and perceives your world from pure love. Not "mind conditioned love," but unconditional "God Love." In this physical world, our focus is usually from the conditioned self and the good, the bad, the happy, the sad all come from the mind as a "State of Mind" following our thought. We add preconceived ideas, attachments and judgments to our every experience.

Studies and experiments by the Military, Philosophers, Physicists and Biologists have now shown again and again that we can activate our dormant genes, affect our level of health, and influence reality in another part of the world through intent focus of the mind. **WOW**. The mind can create dis-ease or health, wealth or poverty, joy or sadness, based upon our beliefs, ideas and thoughts. For many of us, this is the challenge of manifesting our life solely from the mind. Based upon our past experiences, negative and positive, the pattern and belief created, "separate self," can easily shift from a positive or "good thought," resulting from an experience that feels good or trigger to a negative or "bad thought." from an experience that feels bad.

With our choice to adventure into the physical world, our soul will grow and expand in knowledge and wisdom. Along with all the fun, joy, excitement, love and adventures during our amazing time here, each soul chose a challenge or two. Some of us chose to experience more challenges and more growth, and others, less challenges and less growth. All of us create an identity based upon what we most desire to experience! So if you are having a miserable experience in an area of your life, you can dare to overcome it! This is the joy of our adventure!

The beauty of life is that
WE CAN
UNLEARN
all that
LIMITS US!

There are six items that define the Human Mind Ego:

- *All Thoughts*
- *All Concepts*
- *All Perceptions*
- *All Beliefs*
- *All States of Mind*
- *All Reactions*

This is your EGO, Your **"Separate Self Identity."**

***

BECOME AWARE

The mind is the molder of our 3D physical experience. Looking out into the world, the mind sees and believes that everything in the physical is separate from you. To your mind, the trees, animals, and people all have their own identity. The mind places value on each object in the world based upon a belief system. A story. A perception. A belief. *This forms your relationship to the physical experience.* Please take this in. You see what you believe you will see and what the mind has been conditioned to see.

The deeper truth, as Physics and Spirituality reveal, is that there is no separation between people, the world and the Universe, and we are all at our most basic level, ONE. Physics points out, everything breaks down to atoms and molecules, and further into energy. Spiritual philosophy declares, the spirit in us is connected to the spirit in every other thing, living or otherwise. It's all energy. Pretty Deep!

Depending upon what level we look at the world then, we either see we are not separate from, but rather a part of God, (the omniscient, omnipotent being we have been taught is up there somewhere), a part of the Universe, the plants, the world and each other... or we see that *I* am separate from *you*, God and everything else in this physical existence. The point I am making is that the Ego mind views the world from the perspective of *separation*.

SPIRITUALITY AND QUANTUM PHYSICS DECLARE:

There are infinite possibilities available to us and the physical does not exist until we declare it, choose it, and focus the mind on it. Radical and Beyond Deep!

*So, what is **real?***

According to Physics and Spirituality, real is the spirit or the observer, the soul in the physical body that carries on after death. This is the part of us that never changes. Our Soul, or Divine Essence chose to have this amazing experience in the physical and expand the universe.

While living in the physical and through focusing thought, we then determine if life is beautiful, amazing and abundant if we believe and focus on that. Or we determine life is painful, depressing and a struggle if we believe and focus on that! It's all about what you were trained and taught to believe. And this is extremely important!

Let's go Quantum for a moment. Quantum Physics is the study of huge amounts of energy in very small spaces. Through these experiments, Quantum **Physicists have discovered that matter as we understand it is not all that we once believed.**

In Quantum experiments where physicists have studied the atom, they observed the nucleus of the atom and a huge field of energy surrounding the nucleus. This field of energy around the nucleus is best described as a huge wave of "possibilities." As physicists studied the electron in this huge field of energy, in an attempt to measure it and observe it, they found the moment they focused on the electron, that huge amount of energy around the nucleus went from a field of "possibilities," a huge wave - and collapsed into a particle. This is a Quantum event called, the *"Collapsing the Wave Function."* The Physicists, by focusing *their mind* on the electron, found what once was a huge field of energy or infinite "possibilities," then collapsed into a particle, or physical matter. In other words, by focusing their mind on the electron, all of the energy, or the wave of "possibilities," turned into a single particle of matter! The moment the Physicists took their attention off, or their mind off the electron, the huge wave of energy returned and once again became a field of "possibilities."

Through their experiments, Physicists have shown that there are always many possibilities available to us in any moment – which we know from experience is true. During extensive study they also discovered there are atoms popping in and out of existence continually. As soon as they chose to focus on any particle, it became form in a specific position. In short, they found by focusing the mind, possibilities become matter.

*So, what does this have to do **with us?***

Physicists, through their research and experiments confirm what spiritual and metaphysical philosophers have been teaching for centuries. And that is, among many things, we are affecting our world and our experience through what we choose to focus on. If through our focus we are having an effect on molecules and matter, which are the building blocks of our physical world, it seems to reason that through our focus we are also affecting the possibilities of our overall experience.

We have more power and ability to change our world than we have been taught to believe. When we continue to believe and focus on painful thoughts and experiences, the events become a part of our life. As we focus on joyful thoughts and experiences, joyful events and experiences become a part of our life. If we keep viewing our life from the same perspective every day, the same focus, the same prevalent thoughts, our life will essentially, remain the same! Whatever is in our present experience, we will continue to experience! This is why it is so important to be aware of what you focus on consciously or unconsciously each day.

Through your focus (a belief and a thought is also a focus), you are
COLLAPSING
INFINITE FIELDS
OF POSSIBILITY
into the
SAME PATTERNS,
called
YOUR LIFE!

- *Your "story" justifies who you are, what you have been through, what you have become and why you are not as successful or outgoing or abundant as you would like. Your journey out of "Successful Discontent" begins with creating awareness of your story.*

- *If we carry our story forward, through belief systems, our self-talk or repeatedly speaking the story, the energy of the story is brought alive and it becomes yet again a repeated life experience.*

- *Living without an understanding of our personal Ego can cause repetitive pain, or at a minimum, a roller coaster of negative and positive experiences.*

- *Living life from our heart or "Divine Essence" is living without the frustration of a repeating story. We are empowered. We understand the role of the story and our Separate identity. Supportive of a full life, we live each day with awareness, able to choose joy, without judgment of ourselves or our experience.*

- *Through your focus, you are collapsing infinite fields of possibility into the same patterns, called your life! Be mindful of what you focus on.*

⇩

See Workbook for
Activities and Exercises

* * *

CHAPTER 9

Love
THYSELF

The 4 Part Quantum Leap process begins with understanding our Separate Self Identity — our prevalent thought and behavior patterns, our beliefs and stories — and then reveals the importance of Self-Acceptance, Self-Trust and Self-Love to empower our journey. Through awareness, we enable ourselves to get clear on intentions, forgive others as well as ourselves and propel our life to the Heart centered End Results we desire. Integrating this wisdom is life transforming and key to living beyond our discontent - to become empowered and healthy. The final component, is the realization of our own power and *"Coming Home"* to our authentic and true, magnificent self. That Divine self has always been there, but our clouded thinking and lack of education has kept us from it. We are so much more than we believe. We are an absolute miracle, and I am so grateful for my journey and the prayers answered to transform my life and bring this wisdom to you.

God Love Begins With **Love of Thyself**

Loving yourself seems like an easy concept. In order to flow through life and live successfully, it's imperative to love yourself. To embody joy and live fulfilled naturally follow. It's hard to describe the confidence and courage that comes from loving self. To put it in words, it's knowing the world is always working in your favor, miracles do follow miracles and *God is always on your side.*

Many of us do not love who we are and I have found this step to be more important than any amount of positive thinking! Let's look at the idea of loving yourself from a few different perspectives.

Since we were young, we have been taught that we have flaws. In school we did well in some subjects and not so well in others. At home as children we learned patterns of thought from our parents -- from their beliefs and patterns, troubles and pain. As a society, we compare ourselves to others, and to all of the beautiful, intelligent people on TV and in the media, causing us to feel less than. And from our religious upbringing, many of us were taught that we are a sinner in the eyes of God and we will be punished.

We have all done silly things throughout our life. For some of them, we were punished. Some of them we got away with but we forever have them in our memory. Instead of viewing these events as part of our fun and amazing journey and excepting and integrating the wisdom in our experience, we are taught to judge ourselves for things we have done.

If you were traumatized as a child, it's even more difficult. The Separate Self Identity really believes something about you based upon this treatment and until you see the beauty in these events and shift your thought, you will re-affirm your belief through people, places and events throughout your life.

Recall my previously-mentioned childhood stories of being grabbed from behind. Through the shock and pain of those incidents, I created a spiral of unhelpful questions — *what did I do wrong, what's the matter with me, why did this happen, why would someone who was supposed to love me treat me this way* — which my Ego was quick to answer with equally unhelpful and diminishing responses — *you must not be lovable, you did something wrong, you must have deserved it.*

From this perspective it's very difficult to love yourself, to see your value, to live empowered and confident. We carry around with us so much heavy knowledge, judgments and attachments, it's hard to live fulfilled and free, find the love we seek and fill that hole in our heart. We have never been taught the truth about who we are, how we work, the magnificent being we are, and all that we are capable of.

It can be done. Through understanding, accepting and loving yourself just as you are and releasing any lingering self judgment. By understanding and choosing a higher perspective of life, your perfect journey, and the wisdom you are making available to yourself through every experience. You and I chose to arrive in the physical world at this perfect time and place to find joy and excel past our perceived limits.

Sometimes this is hard to see, but if we start to adapt a new viewpoint — *that life is always working perfectly* — we will look for the answers to our own problems, challenges and stressors within ourselves. We must decide to look at life differently, stop getting distracted by our addictions and become aware of what we are attempting to show ourselves through our experience. Once we move an unconscious experience into conscious awareness we then have the ability to direct our mind to higher wisdom, higher thought and higher focus!

If we want consistent success, joy and unwavering abundance, it is important to shift and learn to love every experience. This creates awareness, removes fear and puts us on a path to fully love and accept ourselves.

*Here are three **powerful first steps to loving self.***

STEP 1: ACCEPT WHAT IS – LOVE WHAT IS

Loving what is, is an amazing place to be! In loving what is - we love our life! Given all the situations we may find ourselves in, this can be a huge leap for some of us. If we simply can't love what is, then start with *accepting* what is. Our thought and belief are the molder of our experience. When we can accept that our experience is for our own growth, we begin to awaken to our own power.

As difficult as it is to see in the moment, wherever we may be, if we cannot or do not accept where we are, or better yet, love where we are, we are fighting against the entire universe and we are going to lose the battle. Discontent, irritation, and frustration are usually present when we do not accept or love what is. To live empowered, Its important to accept the perfection of this moment, and exactly what brought us to where we stand today.

You have made choices based upon your belief system and either followed your conditioned Ego, most likely seeking to serve a belief system or you have followed our heart to serve the world. Which do you believe would lead you to joy and a life you easily accept and love?

By accepting and loving where we are, we love ourselves. Through our own choices, we are exactly where we should be. Understanding this, we understand our power and magnificence and know we can change where we are, or any experience we choose. If our situation doesn't feel good, then we take a step back, and understand why we brought this experience into our life. We grow from it and through our own power, choose something different.

When we make choices from a love of self and a love for all, we choose beyond the Ego attempt to be all for ourselves. Beyond the Ego chatter there is peace. Real prosperity becomes an integral part of our life. Tremendous joy and peace come from serving yourself as you serve the world.

STEP 2: OVERCOME YOUR FEAR.

The Separate Self is constantly in fear. We are here to experience growth, but our fear holds us back from living the life we deeply desire. The fear of what others might think of you, the fear of not being good enough, the fear of failure.

On the other side of our fear is great success. When we comprehend the perfection of life and the joy of living, we understand the Ego identity and all the fearful and negative concepts, perceptions, beliefs, and patterns are what limit us from our full potential. This worldly physical experience is only temporary and therefore the Ego is temporary. The Separate Self Ego lives in fear, the fear of dying, the fear of not doing it right, and the fear of what others think.

Fears become real through beliefs. There are three universal fears that affect most of us and cause a reaction of the Separate Self. Let's move these fears to our conscious awareness.

The Ego's Universal Fears are:

- **A Fear of not being Valuable, not worthy, not good enough.** A fear of not having enough, that you are not enough, or you are unworthy of receiving. A feeling that you just do not fit in, or have experiences which you cannot control due to lack of understanding of your own power.

- **A Fear of not Trusting.** Non-trust in your own power and or love of self and your ability to surrender to your heart or Divine essence. A lack of trust in your ability to manifest your reality for the highest and best healing within self. Lack of trust in yourself, Source, God and the process of life.

- **A Fear of Rejection or Abandonment.** Feeling alone, alienated or not a part of. This fear is from an erroneous belief that someone has abandoned you or you have abandoned someone. This fear stems from a false belief in separation from others, Source, God or the Universe.

Most of us have one or more of these fears at play in our life. As long as we operate from our Ego, we attach great value to our Separate Self Identity and live in fear of losing something, someone, or all of what we have. Possessions, people, love – when we fear, we experience a lack of love and acceptance of our value, power and worthiness. Please remember, what we focus on becomes our experience. If we focus on fear, or think fearful thoughts, it is the same as focusing on something we desire, we are summoning this into our reality. Many of us, taking direction from the Separate Self, live in fear each day, causing undo stress and ultimately effecting our health.

In becoming aware of our fears, it's important that we don't judge ourselves. Become aware and uncover the wisdom without judgment. Take all the time you need to become aware of your experiences and fears.

STEP 3: DISCOVER POWER IN FORGIVENESS

To forgive will change everything. At various times in my life, my experiences revealed much anger toward my parents, my ex-wife, my job, and my siblings, to name a few. I re-affirmed my anger and irritation through many daily events, and I became addicted to the emotional response. It started at a young age and throughout my life, I had no real awareness of the degree of anger or where it came from. Even though I was quite successful,

I created an unhealthy emotional bond between myself and my job, my life and many of the people in it. At one point I would awake and think of one miserable thought after another, but managed to put on the happy face when out in public. Many of the people in my daily life could see I was not happy and my reactions would lead people to believe I wasn't a very nice guy. I was patterned. I had a story. I was addicted to it.

From where I stand today, my life has been an amazing and empowering journey. From where I stood back then, I truly believed there were many people that had "done me wrong!" Have you had experiences where people have said and done things that hurt you? Upset you and irritated you? Speaking from a higher perspective, they have had an upbringing that created who *they* are — perfectly. They have a Separate Self and believe they are justified in being who they are. Maybe their Separate Self is addicted to pain and they reaffirm this in their life through their experiences. Maybe they believe they had a horrible childhood and they believe things about themselves that are not true. Our challenge is to see them differently and become aware of the mirror they are to us. The higher truth in our experience with them is to be free of judgment and see all of these experiences with love.

What did my Dad teach me by being who he was? Many things. He taught me to be strong, confident and stand up for myself. He taught me how to love myself for exactly who I am. He taught me to step into my own power. To honor and value myself. Ultimately, he brought me to perfect self-awareness which taught me to stop believing my old patterns of self doubt and self judgment.

Until I learned this, I was caught in a roller coaster experience of good and bad, happy then sad. I was living life patterned after him. I was angry inside, hurt and discouraged. I did my best to hide it and stuff it, and it continued to show itself in many disempowering ways. As hard as it was, I learned to see my Dad for who he was. He really thought I was somebody I wasn't, based upon his own belief system. A belief system of what he believed *he* was.

*This is living life from **the Ego.***

We really believe we are right and we react constantly to our own life experience.

To see the gift in our experience, to see the beautiful wisdom that we are showing ourselves and to integrate it, changes everything. This is the basis for forgiveness. When we can acknowledge the deeper truth and forgive the people our Ego mind believes caused our pain, we let go of the resentment, the anger, the guilt, and the constant discontent.

The spiritual wisdom here is that no one can cause you pain. We cause *our own pain.* If you didn't believe it, it would not create a reaction within you. Spiritually speaking, the people in our lives are perfect mirrors and actors in our own play, here on earth teaching us how to be whole. They show up in perfect timing and in perfect ways to reveal our vulnerabilities.

In the case of my Dad, before we came to this world we decided to have this experience together. I wrote the script, handed it to him and I asked him to read it to me. My Dad read the script perfectly. I could wallow in pain or choose to grow. By facing this generation after generation of recurring suffering and pain, following generations will be free of the experience.

As I did my forgiveness process many years ago, I came to realize one beautiful piece of wisdom. My Dad had felt a lack of love all his life. So many of us do. He was hurt and did his best to hide it. Today with all my heart I can say, "I forgive you Dad. From this day forward, I send you nothing but love. Thank you for your gift."

*This **dissolves the pain** with him.*

*So how do we **forgive?***

If we have deep seated anger or resentment, grief or sadness, it must come out. The feelings and emotions must be expressed and understood — or we wrestle with them throughout our life, causing pain, suffering and finally dis-ease.

*Here's a simple but **powerful,***
5-STEP
"FORGIVENESS"
PROCESS
I love to use with clients:

1. Begin by becoming aware of every person, place or thing in your life that you believe did you harm. If it's hard to think about, ask for guidance and help. You have beautiful light beings who want to support you. Guides. Angels. Masters. We all do.

2. Grab a notepad and write. Put all the people down on paper who you believe hurt you. What happened? How did they hurt you? It's important to see how they made you feel. Bring awareness to all of the events. Get it all out of you and on to paper — all of it.

3. Then yell, scream, cuss and express this out loud. ALL OF IT. Take as long as it takes. One month or six months, it doesn't matter. Take each event and each person, one at a time, and process.

4. Once all of the emotions are out, ask yourself, from a higher perspective, what is it that this person taught me? See the person from a soul perspective. What did I learn? What did this soul really want for me? Where is this pain holding me back? What is the deeper, higher truth? One by one, when you can see the person or event with love and acceptance, you are on your way to forgiveness.

5. The last and most important step is understanding your part in the events and forgiving yourself. Ultimately, it's you that you must forgive. To shift your life and let go of this anchor, this huge piece of negative energy, that has most likely been causing havoc with your happiness and success, you must understand your part in this experience. Own up to what you believe. The thoughts

you have. Your story. There is wisdom there. Bringing this knowledge from the unconscious mind to conscious awareness will bring tears of pain and tears of joy. And ultimately, will change what the mind believes to be true, which will change your life!

The Spiritual truth:
*Your soul **chose** this.*
You wanted this experience to grow beyond it.

WHAT DID YOU LEARN?

This is huge in terms of living authentically and understanding your own power. It is a first step in understanding your value, how you have brought experiences into your life, and what you have been attempting to tell yourself for years. It leads to amazing breakthroughs and many find a voice they have never had. We are led to trust in ourselves and in our own abilities as we, for the first time, see that we were always loved and all the old beliefs and stories are tossed aside. Awareness of our part in the experience leads us to confidently create new experiences, while letting go of the thoughts and beliefs that had us living in fear, judgment and lack.

BASIC STEPS TO LOVING YOURSELF

Loving yourself is about honoring your desires, following your passions and accepting that what you desire most is what the universe wants for you.

The following are some helpful basic questions and ideas for embarking on your journey to self-love.

- *What lights you up inside? Identify things, people, and events. What do you really want?* Without guilt or shame. Give it to yourself. Go for it! Know you deserve it. All it takes is a commitment from you. This creates tremendous joy.

- *Where do you like to go?* Visit and enjoy.

- *What are your favorite foods?* Bon Appetite.

- *Who is in your life that challenges you?* Love what they show you. Learn. Embrace it, without an Ego reaction. Learn to accept and love where you are and what you experience.

- *Be acutely aware of your patterns and thoughts. Be able to look at what you react to and choose to learn from it, without judgment of the event, person or yourself.* When you understand and integrate the wisdom without reaction, it stops showing up. *Pivot. Choose differently. Without blaming.*

- **Cultivate a knowing of how magnificent you are.**
  You are a part of God. God is a part of you. The world is
  working in your favor. Once you cast off what the ego
  believes — You cannot lose.

- **Be aware of everyone else in your life and the realization that they also have their own journey.** Let them
  have it. If you perpetuate judgment toward others, you
  also perpetuate judgment toward yourself.

- **Every day for 30 days or as long as it takes, look in the mirror and tell yourself all the wonderful things you accomplished that day.** State your successes. Conclude
  with looking yourself straight in the eye and tell yourself
  lovingly, "I love you _____." "I love and approve of you
  _____." Use your name in the statement. Continue as
  long as necessary. If you are doing this with heartfelt
  emotion and it brings a tear to your eye, you are doing it
  correctly.

- **Create intentions to get clear on where you want to go in life and take the steps to make them happen!**

- **Recognize the mind, the Ego when it speaks.** Be acutely
  aware of the self-judgments and the attachments to who
  you believe you should be. Remember, the Ego is conditioned and it cannot wrap itself around all you can have
  or all you can become. There are infinite possibilities for
  your life, and your Divine Essence knows this.

- *By accepting and loving where we are, - and everything that brought us to where we are - we love ourselves. We understand our magnificence and know we can change any experience.*

- *The Ego's universal fears are – the fear of not being good enough, the fear of not trusting, and the fear of rejection or abandonment. As long as we operate from our Ego, we live in fear of losing something, someone, or all that we have.*

- *To see the gift and the beautiful wisdom in our experience, and to integrate it, changes everything. This is the basis for forgiveness.*

- *The last and most important step in the forgiveness process is understanding your part in the events and forgiving yourself. Ultimately, it's you that you must forgive.*

- *Cultivate a knowing of how magnificent you are. You are a part of God. God is a part of you. The world is working in your favor. You cannot lose.*

See Workbook for
Activities and Exercises

{ CHAPTER 10 }

***

DEFINE *Your* END RESULT

We've learned how powerful it is to focus the mind. And that what we choose to focus on becomes our experience. Now let's learn about using the mind and the heart together to create a fun, fulfilling and rewarding life.

Having a fulfilling life starts with connecting to your heart's desire and focusing on the end result. I love the idea of placing our focus on the end result. The journey to our heart's desire then becomes an adventure we *love*. The more we take steps in the direction of our dream, happily trusting and allowing life to unfold, we combine the power of our heart's intention with the all-knowing Divine Essence to take us down a path of amazing experiences. Many of my clients experience fun and adventurous lives as they weave their way to their intended end result. The rewards are huge if we stay focused, take steps toward our dream, and trust in the ultimate outcome.

Did I ever predict that I would be teaching? No. Did I know that I would end up teaching this subject matter? No. I do remember my days back in College when I loved mentoring the other students. They caught on quick. It was extremely rewarding, and so much fun! Yet, I ended up doing what I was schooled to do for years, without a real passion for it, always feeling like there was something else I was better suited for. It wasn't until I totally let go of my death grip on my corporate job, and what I thought was "Safe" and "Right" that I weaved my way to a perfect career, a wonderful income and an inspiring life.

The Ego can be a very powerful force, and at a young age it will dominate your thoughts with what you have been taught to believe. Most of us get trapped here and never break free. If I can make an impact on your life right now, I would highly advise you stop whatever you are doing that doesn't feel good, get quiet and begin to listen to your heart. It is from this place that I want you to create intentions for your life. The how and the way will be shown to you in perfect timing.

I have witnessed many people — business owners, investors and celebrities — create an experience they were taught to create, believing it will make them happy. The brilliant piece of knowledge here is found in the statement — *stop focusing outside of yourself to find happiness!* The house, the car, a job, the bank account can be fun and a part of your dream, but will not create happiness and will eventually leave you flat. It's important to address the patterns of old addictive thoughts, beliefs and feelings, and cultivate trust in yourself to create the life you REALLY want, or your ultimate result will be some level of success, that includes Successful Discontent.

How do we bring limitless possibilities and the life we desire and resonate with into our experience? It's a process of getting past the limiting thoughts and concepts you have been taught, following the heart and focusing the mind to make your ultimate life a reality.

Here are the steps:

1. Define and set your intention on an End Result that resonates with you and creates joy.

2. Take 10 minutes daily to use your imagination and visualize your End Result feeling the joy of your dream come true.

3. Trust in the outcome and in your ability to make your dream a reality. Take action toward your End Result, and get out in the world with faith. Most of all, choose to be happy, and have fun while you witness the synchronicities and serendipities unfold!

4. Let go of any doubt! Follow your joy.

5. Stay focused and "Allow" each next step to unfold. Know that in Divine perfect timing and in perfect ways your End Result will materialize.

YOU HAVE A BEAUTIFUL *DIVINE ESSENCE.*

This is your connection to God and the realm that does not see right or wrong, good or bad, but perfection. All is perfect in Gods world. As you learn the tendencies of your Separate Self Ego and learn to watch the mind carefully, choosing empowering thought, it becomes easier and easier to stay in your heart and cultivate the connection to your Essence. Your Divine Essence encompasses your soul. Your soul is the reason you are here in the physical and is only interested in love, growth and expansion. The Soul does not cause pain. The Divine Essence does not judge or attach any of Ego beliefs or limiting behaviors to anything you wish to create. Manifesting any desire from the heart and soul will in perfect timing and perfect ways create a result that is highest and best for you, and the world.

Divine Essence always knows what is best for you and stimulates tremendous happiness in the process! Through our heart-focused intentions, we can create a career that uplifts us and our life as a whole, relationships that are highest and best for us that create growth, love and connection, and from a Divine perspective we can create abundance by being in the flow and serving ourselves as we serve others.

The conditioned Ego mind and our belief system is the only part of the equation that can bring pain and disruption into the process. Your Soul is well aware of your perceived challenges and knows whatever you experience in life will give you the opportunity for the growth you desire. That's why you are here. Your family, your choices, the events of your life are revealing exactly what you want to change. You can either push it away and choose to ignore the challenge, hoping it will disappear, or face it and learn. The key is to recognize what you react to, take ownership of your thoughts and patterns, and shift your focus. Then create knowing intentions and allow the Divine peace and creation to occur!

This is how LIFE WORKS. **PERFECTLY.** *Perfect for our growth.* LIFE IS **PERFECTION.**

If we address our beliefs and patterns that we are learning through, we are poised for expansion and growth. We all have a perfect journey. It's up to us what we do with it!

***

HOW TO CREATE WITH HEART, MIND AND SOUL

I am going to challenge you to let go of the old notion of goal setting. Does setting goals work? Yes. If you focus on your goal and let yourself be led to taking action, many goals will become a reality. Remember, what we focus the mind on becomes our experience.

*It will **show up!***
But – it will show up with your
***beliefs** around it intact.*

In one of my "spiritual" trainings, we talked about goal setting the old-school way: "SMART" goals. SMART stands for specific, measurable, attainable, relevant, and time bound. In any goal or intention process, it is always good to get clear on your desire, engage the imagination with feeling and take action steps in the direction of your desire. But in the eyes of the Universe using SMART GOAL SETTING can be *limiting*.

*Here are some examples of **Goals set** using*
THE SMART METHOD:

1. Profession/Career Goal: I am a computer software engineer, earning a salary of $200,000 a year, utilizing my education and talent to create programs for a major computer software company by 6pm CST on or before December 1st, Year X.

2. Relationship Goal: I have a beautiful relationship with a 40-year-old cute blonde woman. She is spiritual, successful, healthy, has a great career and income, is family oriented and loves to travel. We create a great life together. She and I are dating and sharing our life by 12 noon CST on or before January 31st Year X.

3. Personal (Residence) Goal: I live in a 3,000 square foot or larger modern ranch home with a professionally landscaped yard with a beautiful chef's kitchen with white cabinets, large master bedroom and master bathroom, 25 x 20 office with built-in bookcases. The house is in great condition and equipped with an outdoor pool and hot tub and a lower level game room. The home is priced at $600,000 or less and located in Santa Barbara, California. I purchase the home by 3pm CST on or before July 1, Year X.

These are all great examples of
S.M.A.R.T. GOALS.

Yet several questions come up when creating these goals.

- First and foremost is there any belief system or pattern in the way of attaining the goal?

- Is this goal believable consciously and unconsciously?

- Does the goal align with your deeper purpose?

- How does the goal resonate with you?

- Do you sing with joy in your heart as you read the goal?

*For me, when I read these goals I feel **tension and fear!***

Let's take a look at the career goal. Many people choose and define a career that may initially seem exciting and worthwhile, only to find once the career is attained, there are many factors that don't support their hearts desires.

The range of objections is broad:

- The work is not rewarding or fun.

- The role they choose may limit their decision making and controls their creativity.

- They do not have enough freedom to live life fully outside of work.

- The work is demanding and the hours are awful.

- The job is not what they thought it would be, and on and on.

The soul wants to expand and is not fulfilled! Basic needs are not met. The Ego may be getting what it wants (ie., a desirable income or respect from peers), but we long for something more. Old patterns and old stories of the Ego mind that are not healed will show up in whatever we do or through the mirrors in our lives. Ultimately, the journey toward our intention should be fun and create joy! To live in upheaval or mediocrity is not our soul's choice.

Working with SMART goals defines what we believe is our desire, but we would have a hard time defining our perfect experience. There are all sorts of objections that come about regarding the above relationship goal and the personal goal.

- What if the woman appears for you, but her great job has her working on weekends or nights?

- What if the woman does not appear by January 31, year X? Or must work in another state?

- What happens if the woman has several of her own children and you struggle with kids?

- Let's say we are working near Santa Barbara, we purchase a home there only to find another "perfect" home in a neighboring town…

- or in a few months the absolutely earth-shatteringly perfect career shows up in San Francisco?

SO MANY *WHAT-IFS!*

The point I wish to make is that by being so specific with our goals, it creates a lot of stress to bring this specific something by a specific date! What happens if the goal does not manifest by the date specified? More stress? What story will your mind make up or turn into a belief if the goal doesn't appear? Have you failed? Do you suffer with doubt or discouragement? These goals create a perfect opportunity for "Successful Discontent."

By creating goals of this nature, we are defining life through our Ego and our present situation. The absolute limitless possibilities for your life, and *the absolute limitless possibilities of the universe are now limited!*

In being too specific with our goal, we are actually thinking small and leaving out our ability to manifest with Divine perfection. We can create anything! When creating from our Essence, we intend from the heart and Soul without a need to control the outcome. We stay focused and we feel Joy. We allay fear and know and trust the relationship, the career, the personal intentions will all come together in perfect timing and in perfect ways.

Your Essence knows of the perfect job for you, perfect home for you, perfect partner for you!

* * *

INFINITE POSSIBILITIES

Please understand this!
There are
INFINITE
POSSIBILITIES
available to you.

We are not raised to think that way. In effect, by using SMART goals, we are creating resistance to the creative power of the universe and life's inherent magic!

Your Beloved may not be blonde. Your dream job may not be the one with the corner office. Your wealth is not just money. When we can completely surrender our desire and trust it will show up perfectly, it will.

There is another way! A fantastic awesome way to bring into your life, the joy, the peace, and the perfection of your heart's deepest desires. The Divinely orchestrated and inspired life can bring you all that you want and fulfill your every dream!

My experience and training taught me a process that is by far much more rewarding, fulfilling and successful. It does not require that you become stressed out or doubtful in the creation process. This is the process of creating intentions that feel fantastic and awaken your soul! Done correctly, they will not cause stress or anxiety in the process of creating the life you want. They are wide open to Divine creation and thus the limitless possibilities of the universe.

What's most important is how you feel
*in your **intention process!***

The following statements are examples of intending what I desire, feeling joyful, excited and leaving the how-to's and what-if's up to the universe:

- **Relationship:** *I am in a beautiful, fulfilling relationship with a cute, healthy lady. We are fun and playful together. We have beautiful chemistry and we laugh together frequently. We both love to travel and experience awesome adventures in many beautiful areas of the world. She is the perfect lady for me and I am perfect for her. We are happy together. She is spiritual like me, knowing we can be, do or have anything we desire! She really excites me and we create a fun life of joy!*

- **Residence:** *I am so happy and grateful to own a beautiful home on the water! With a beautiful kitchen, beautiful baths, a perfect office space, a fun game room and a fantastic master bedroom all in a tropical paradise! My girl and I love to sit on the deck and watch the waves come into shore.*

- **Personal:** *I am guided to my path of beauty, wisdom and a happy life that feels good! I am a healthy, happy, fun, vibrant, spiritual millionaire!*

- **Career:** *I have creative, fulfilling work that I love! Work that I am best suited for so I can have lots of fun while I work! I am excited, passionate and filled with joy as I serve the world greatly! I am an Outrageously Successful Celebrity Trainer!*

- **Finances:** *I have enough wealth and abundance to easily pay for my beautiful home, to travel the world speaking, educating and serving others and never have to worry about how I will pay for it. As I share wisdom and wealth, I am carefree, experience massive joy and I am free to have lots of fun! There are no limits. I live in the flow of abundance and abundance flows to serve myself, my business and the world!*

The universe responds to your feelings! The intention must resonate greatly with you and create heartfelt joy. These types of intentions are added to or modified from time to time, but always include happiness! For me, if I am happy, it includes a career that astounds me, a relationship that is fun and a happy as well as a prosperous life that serves others while serving myself. The specifics of that do not play into the intention. The feeling of joy and fulfillment is key.

Let the Universe bring to you
SOMETHING BEYOND
what you can even
IMAGINE
for yourself!

Design intentions that feel fantastic, resonate with your heart and Soul. Leave the "how's" wide open and up to the universe!

*Here's how to put this into **practice:***

- Take 15 minutes a day and visualize your End Result while stating your intentions out loud. Release each one of your statements to the universe with excitement and joy and let your Divine Essence bring you what is highest and best for you, the world and your own life journey!

- Attachments, values and judgments are all from the Separate Self. In this process, learn to *surrender* and *allow* your desires to become your reality.

- In order to continue to draw your intention into your life, envision it as already happening, stay in joy and have zero attachment to any of your desires! This means be grateful for what you have, what you experience and the path you are on without doubting the highest and best end result! Accept and love the journey. Be filled with joy! This is how you create a life beyond the judging, fearful separate self ego.

- To place more energy behind your focus, imagine the End Result scene or event in your mind each day with joy and excitement or create a vision board with a photo layout of your desired end results. Check in each day for 10 minutes by envisioning your desired End Result or by viewing your vision board and allowing the excitement to build.

The key to having successful intentions is to be consistent with your dream and trust in the magic as you take steps out in the world and allow the perfect experiences, synchronicities and serendipities to show up. When you begin, it's common to doubt which steps to take, so take any steps that bring you joy. Get involved with groups and events that interest you. Volunteer, show up with joy and gratitude and the Universe will show you the way! When you feel inspired you are on the path to your dreams.

Take time now and create intentions that are fun and create happiness in these areas of your life. Write them so they sing in your heart when you read them!

Write out Your Intentions in *7 Areas of Life:*

- Career/Service
- Relationships/Love
- Financial/Abundance
- Personal
- Health/Fitness
- Recreation/Fun
- Legacy/What You Leave to the World

***

WHY MANY OF US DON'T GET WHAT WE WANT

Consciously we have approximately 60,000 thoughts a day. Most of these thoughts are repetitive. Many cause us to trigger, i.e. to have a powerful emotional reaction. And many of the reactions are negative.

Knowing what we now know, guess what that brings us?

In very basic terms where your attention goes – energy flows.

For example, many of us wake up each morning – with our attention on all the things we have to accomplish. Each day we focus on the people we will see, the job we do, the places we have to go and the objects we own. As we focus on the things we have to do, our mind stays focused on the known and familiar people, places, and things in our life. Unconsciously then, most of us stay in a predictable routine, the body following our thoughts to what is familiar.

As we think of all the places we have to go, the things we have to do and the people we will see, most days are spent in a constant and addictive low level of stress. It becomes easier each day to connect with our old and familiar way of perceiving the world and the emotions that follow. Many of us listen to our Ego and the fears of loosing our job, having the "right" relationship, or paying the mortgage, and we desperately try to control the outcome of our daily experience. As stress and anxiety become a routine experience, we find ourselves in familiar territory again and again, where it's difficult to focus with joy on anything new, different and exciting. The result? Many of us are continually siphoning energy away from all the amazing possibilities available to us, and into a very predictable future.

Furthermore, if we wake up each day and connect with the emotion of unhappiness, futility, pain or stress, the moment we feel this emotion our mind is focused on an event that connects us to the many events from the past where we experienced that familiar emotion. As all emotion is a chemical residue from the past, we once again are no longer focused on possibilities. Sometimes we overcome our old pattern and feel great about an experience, or several experiences. We get "on a roll" which is fantastic, but for most of us it is not sustained. In order to sustain the joy and focus it takes to create something new in our life and to consistently focus on the unknown, we must get beyond our repetitive thinking, our story and reactions to bring a new experience.

Once we begin to repeatedly take time and focus on change, our life will change! Many of us just don't take the time. Why? Depending on our life up to this moment, many of us don't believe we have an affect on reality. We have never been taught how we work, the beautiful purpose of our life and our amazing Divine power. While we attempt to stay positive, because that is what we have been told to do, many of us have a dab of positivity over a mass of old beliefs, stories and patterns that do not serve us, and positive results are rarely sustained.

Think about this for a moment. On any typical day in our life we will place our attention on our job, a coworker, the family, our partner, our parents, our in-laws, our phone, our body, our pain, our joy, the news, Facebook, Instagram, our computer, our kids, the car, money, or lack of money, and one of my favorites, food! Our mind (and many times our heart) remains focused on the known and familiar. This continual focus leaves very little energy to focus our thoughts on amazing possibilities and bring something new into our life.

By investing a small amount of time and attention on your hearts desire, (an End Result that resonates with who you are), and feeling joy as you place your attention on something new, the universe will feel you, serendipities will occur, and you will follow your thoughts to a new experience.

A new
POSSIBILITY
is
POSSIBLE!

- *The first steps toward a fulfilling life include connecting to your heart's desire and creating an intention with a focus on the End Result.*

- *As you learn the tendencies of your Ego and learn to watch the mind carefully, it becomes easier and easier to stay in your heart and create and cultivate the connection to your Essence.*

- *When manifesting from our Essence, we create from the heart without attachment or judgment. We focus and we feel Joy. We allay fear and know and trust the relationship, the career, the personal intentions will all come together in perfect timing and in perfect ways. We allow the universe to bring us more than we can imagine!*

- *Design intentions that feel fantastic, resonate with your Heart and Soul. Leave the "how's" wide open and up to the universe!*

- *By investing our attention and focus daily on something new - with an elevated emotion - we will begin to follow our thoughts to a new experience.*

⇩

See Workbook for
Activities and Exercises

{ CHAPTER 11 }

* * *

How We
SABOTAGE
OUR OWN JOY

AN UNCONSCIOUS FOCUS ON THE PAST STRESSED OUT SARAH

Sarah was having a difficult time sleeping. She was wrestling with disruptive thoughts about her life. She called me one day in a panic just as I was leaving the office. "I *need* to see you; I am so stressed out! Can I come in now?" I could hear the fear in her voice. She wanted to come in that evening and begin working on her *emotional addiction* to anxiety and stress.

Sarah was having difficulty with her life and her family, and it was affecting her health. Sarah's Mom had been very ill and had just passed. She told the story of how she had taken care of her Mom for several months and was currently making all the arrangements for her Mom's services. She felt the loss of someone close to her and she was angry at her siblings for their lack of involvement and support. More importantly, and although Sarah was not yet aware of it, she was angry with herself.

*Sarah was living out an **old pattern.***

Throughout her life she was consistently worried and had experienced heightened stress for many years. She was not able to calm herself and now it had begun to affect her health. She had lost a lot of weight. She didn't sleep well or eat well. It was difficult to numb her pain. To add to her stress and worry, most recently Sarah was told by her doctors and dermatologists that she must limit her outdoor activity to slow the development of spider veins in her face. Sarah was livid. She enjoyed the outdoors and the sun. Her stress was exacerbated by a fear of smiling. Throughout the process of working with Sarah, she would stifle her ability to laugh for fear she would increase the spider veins in her face.

For several reasons and a conditioning from childhood, Sarah was in fear of being herself. Being authentic and walking through life, trusting in her own beauty, talent and magnificence was something she lost in her upbringing. After identifying the causes of her stress and her thought patterns, we mapped out the most powerful process to support her. It was a different approach. The first big step for her was to have gratitude and appreciation for the experiences she was having. She reacted harshly when I first suggested this. "Grateful!? You have got to be kidding!", she exclaimed.

Yes, gratitude.

She grudgingly went along with my suggestion. To begin with, this began to shift her focus. In shifting her focus to gratitude, she began to interrupt the old neural pathway in the brain which connected her to past events and a familiar pain. And in being grateful for her experience, she began to acknowledge her own power to manifest her highest life. She stopped focusing on and blaming all the things outside of herself and released the resistance to her "perfect" life challenges. Why did she believe she must do everything herself, with little support from her family? Why was she so worried and stressed with daily life? Why was she now having an issue with Rosacea and spider veins?

Sarah's challenge began as a child. She had a childhood filled with stress and each of her emotions originated at an early age. Her Father was a controlling man who had bouts of anger and became immobilized and confined to a wheelchair later in life. Her Mother became so stressed in the house that Sarah took on many of the household responsibilities. Throughout her childhood everyone was afraid to speak up and just be themselves. Sarah now patterned after her Mom's anxiety and stress and as her Mom had done, she held her real feelings in. Other than an occasional explosion of frustrated thoughts, Sarah experienced resentment and did not express herself well in social situations or with her siblings. She exhausted herself in attempting to keep life light and under control. She believed she was the one who had to take care of chores, make decisions and handle unexpected events.. She did not believe in or trust in her own ability to create the life she wanted and wallowed in stress, discouragement and patterned her Mother and Fathers behaviors. Her continual pattern of stress and anger was now having an effect on Sarah's health. It was immobilizing. At times she was paralyzed with fear. She believed she was a victim.

When Sarah began to acknowledge the patterning of her Mom and Dad, life began to change. She recognized that she chose to support her Mom. She was not forced her take these actions. She became aware of her unhealthy choices and her lack of expressing her desires, feelings, and requests for support and fulfillment. Having had this pattern since childhood was now causing her deep frustration. She also became aware of, how she despised doing things she didn't enjoy. She was able to work through her fear of speaking up and without resentment or anger, she asked for support with her choice to perform tasks and duties. As a result, she found supportive groups, and people took a more active role to assist Sarah.

Sarah uncovered her hidden challenges and learned to let go of her Ego's need to control outcomes. Her pattern of keeping everything under control was rooted in keeping her safe. During her upbringing she learned to keep the peace by quickly taking care of what needed attention. Throughout the Quantum Leap Program, we worked together to create new opportunities and heart driven end results. Sarah was overjoyed and uncovered a new ability to trust in the perfection of life. More powerfully, she began believing and trusting in herself and her ability to live the life she desired.

*Sarah was able to see a **higher truth.***

She was able to calm her mind and break the bonds to her addictive repetitive feelings. While uncovering her old story, she owned up to her part in the events of her life and began to appreciate the repetitive experiences, even the ones that her Ego would label "bad." Sarah started listening to and acting from her Essence. She learned to love herself and her journey, which changed her life. For the first time in many years, Sarah was able to allow herself to have fun, appreciate what she was showing herself and was surprised at how much better she was able to sleep at night! The last time I saw Sarah, she was smiling from ear to ear and had just finished telling me how herself and her husband had purchased a place in sunny Arizona. They fly out each winter and explore the landscape.

Many of us take a very different approach and wrestle with our monkeys all of our life. We continually complain and blame, re-hash our old story again and again or even worse, we yell at the people in our life, kick the dog and get upset with ourselves. And the negative energy remains.

* * *

BE GRATEFUL

"Make gratitude a part of your day. Appreciate and love your life, and life will love you back."
– ME

From this day forward, we must

ASK OURSELVES
to
SEE LIFE
THROUGH A NEW LENS.

When we choose gratitude for the life we have, we claim our power. What are we to be grateful for? The opportunites and wisdom that our experience provides and our ability to shift our focus. Anxiety and an overactive mind usually reveal a lack of understanding, or a lack of trust in yourself and a lack of knowing who you really are and your power to change. When we react to a person place or event, we reveal something our Separate Self believes to be true or desires to change. There is wisdom in the experience for you to become aware of. Take the first powerful step today. Be grateful for the experience and appreciate it! The more we appreciate all the situation reveals, the faster we remove unhealthy thoughts and heal ourselves.

***

YOU'RE A MAN, ACT LIKE ONE

Abundance, especially money can be a hot topic for many people. Men grow up with ideas around money. Women have their ideas about money too.

We all deserve to have it, and to share it with others. Why do so many of us live in lack and scarcity? Beliefs. Patterns. Programming.

Relationships can show us so many things about ourselves. I have learned so much from my relationships, it astounds me still. A few years back I had an intention to have an amazing loving relationship. Here was my intention.

I have the most beautiful, playful, fun, loving, kind, *deeply connected* relationship with a woman I have ever had! We laugh together frequently! We have fantastic chemistry! She is Spiritual like me ..and so, so cute! She really gets me and she is my perfect mate and travel partner!

At this particular time, I also had an intention regarding my life. I desired to be taught all I need to know, the deeper wisdom to get beyond my patterns, my beliefs and stories, to enable myself to live in joy and be free to choose whether I would return to this physical world and experience another life, or not return and be of greater support to the physical world through work in the non-physical realm. During my trainings with Enlightened Masters I was given the knowledge that we, (our energy, or soul, in another physical body) can return to the physical world as the eyes and ears of God, or not return. Many of us have had many lifetimes and experiences to grow our soul, but that is an entirely different book.

If you wish to learn more regarding this concept I will mention two books. The first being a book written by a highly educated and prominent Psychiatrist, Dr. Brian Weiss M.D.

entitled, "Many Lives, Many Masters." And the second book written by Anita Moorjani entitled, "Dying to Be Me."

In any relationship, both parties have patterns, beliefs and stories. Depending on your intention and desire, your relationship can show you a little growth, a medium amount of growth or lots of growth! Some relationships yield very little growth and the soul starves for more. In my case, did I have a deeply connected relationship? YES! Did we laugh together frequently? YES! Did we have fantastic chemistry? Absolutely! Being that my intention was to learn how to get beyond my limiting and negative patterns and thoughts, I have experienced massive growth in my close relationships!

When my girl and I first met she was struggling financially. At this time in my life, that did not matter, I had a great income and savings so we traveled to far off lands, experienced radical adventures, and pretty much went wherever we chose to go. It was beautiful and fun. I was also building another business and spending massive amounts of cash on my entrepreneurial education. We flew here and there, soaked up the sun, experienced great food, great people and lots of adventure! Loads of fun, right?

There was a problem. After several years of this lifestyle, I realized I had not placed the focus on the business that is required to create the *"unknown"* I desired, and I lacked the massive success to keep up with my current "adventure." When I came to this realization, I panicked! I slammed on the brakes and our lifestyle took a huge turn. In short, my savings and income were something I needed to refocus on as well as building my service-oriented business with joy!

And it must happen NOW.

I created new intentions around my income and abundance that were similar to the wealth and abundance intention examples above. Slowly but surely, just as I expected, my wealth began to grow, but I went through a period of stress and self-judgment for getting myself in this position.

Prior to my panic situation, my girl had been quietly and consistently building her business. She was feeling great about all she was doing and worked her way into a position to support herself well, which leads me to the point of the story.

After spending so much of my income and savings on many trips, flights, meals, creating a home, etc. – I hate to admit this – but I (my Separate Self) had become triggered. Even though I chose to do these things, I chose to adventure and explore, and I had made each and every choice, I was now upset. As much as I tried to tell myself I allowed this, I chose to have these experiences, I didn't like where I was - where I had taken myself - and my mind would "make up" that she now "had it made" and here I was struggling! And once my mind found one item to focus on that wasn't working, it would find many more, as this is what most minds will do. The stories were amazing and frequent as my Ego mind did its best to defray responsibility for my own actions. To top it all off, due to my judgmental behavior and the lack I wrestled with, the relationship was now in a different place and we struggled.

From the very beginning of our relationship we could always easily connect with each other. She could always tell where I was emotionally-speaking, and I could tell where she was, even if we were not together. (My deeply connected intention at work!)

My girl could tell I was not in a, "happy place!" As I continued to focus on and build my new business, one day, we decided to meet for lunch. We did the usual chatting, it was fun, but then something different happened. During the meal she gave me a check to offset some of the expenses I had incurred. She said she could tell I was upset and struggling. I was speechless. As I sat there, attempting to decide what to do, my Ego went straight to my old belief system.

You are a man, act like one!

The Separate Self Identity believed, this is not the way it works! I am the provider and I can't take money from you. It may be old school, but being a man, raised how I was raised, the man did the providing. It was embarrassing, humiliating and deeply gratifying all at the same time. When I snapped back to reality, I told myself she has her own expenses, she has children to feed, and almost immediately, acting like a man, I rejected the offer.

But, my Ego was clinging to the story, "I always give, give, give and I don't get much back." Maybe its time for you to receive? I wrestled with my beliefs and stories for weeks. The Ego is a master at disguises. Sometimes a resentful thought would show up and I would want to cash the check. And then I would tell myself, make your own money Michael, you don't need hers. I was in a place of real gratitude and grace for her offer. But, I didn't want to accept the check.

During the events of one quick lunch I revealed a lot about myself. I came to the realization it had always been difficult for me to receive. And, when I made the decision to give, I would give, give talent, give time, give my abundance, and over time a resulting pattern of feeling taken advantage of would appear. I also came to realize I had an expectation when I decided to give. And I would allow myself to be disappointed when I didn't receive something in return.

I became aware. Going forward, if I decide to give, I give freely with a smile and allow the experience. I had given to many all my life. And having made my own way and created my own success, I had become very independent. Now in one quick moment, I was in 'no mans" land. What a story. The Ego, the beliefs and patterns at work.

How did I get here? Again, it was easy. I had set intentions to create wealth and abundance, to be in a flow of abundance and serve the world, my business and myself. But a check from my girl was not the form I expected. Based upon my beliefs, I expected something else. New clients, speaking engagements, seminars, that would be ok. The universe and my soul were giving me just what I asked for and I was turning it away.

By turning this gift away, I stopped the flow of abundance and I stopped myself from feeling abundant and loved! I did not give my girl the chance to complete this cycle, the cycle of - I gave, she received, she gave, I received. The higher truth - as much as I wanted to, it was not my place to worry about her abundance or her decision. Worry did not support her. And where is my mind focusing when I worry? Lack of. And what is my mind bringing?

Lack of. She was in a beautiful place and had recognized she received from me and now she was giving back.

Grateful for the entire experience, in the end, I did not cash her check. I just could not take from her and her children. If it meant I would struggle for a few more months, so be it. And I did. But, I learned much about myself and it changed my future. I refocused on my intentions to allow an abundant business to form and I learned to love myself enough to accept abundance from any avenue the universe provides. My girl, by offering the check to me, believed in her ability to create further abundance and this became her experience.

Remember, everything in the 3D world is energy. When we give, without a mindset of scarcity or attachment, the Universe returns to us. The return of abundance can take many forms. Unless we stop it, it has to happen. We are all one. Many of us act from lack, believing in the fear of "not enough." Therefore, we restrict ourselves from the perfect flow of life. Money is a big trigger for many a Separate Self. The Ego believes money is power, and without money we are weak. As a child, I lived in this fear of lack for years. Cultivating trust in this process set my life on a new path.

A big lesson here is,
"IN GIVING IS RECEIVING."

Now I was ready to give and receive without stress. And I did. Again, this situation appeared in perfect Divine timing and perfect for my growth.

***

DIVINE PERFECTION

We all wish to enjoy our life and have fun. Becoming aware of our limiting concepts, perceptions and stories expand our ability to experience amazing joy, love and peace! When we understand that through conscious or unconscious thought, we mold our experiences for our own growth and joy, we realize each person, event and result is part of the divine journey of life.

Remember that the Ego mind is the only part of you that frames events into "good" and "bad." From a divine perspective, see it ALL as perfect. You are on a perfect journey and learning perfectly. Appreciate the experience! Accept the experience! Allow yourself the transformation through every experience and let go of any resistance to it.

This may be easier said than done, but with practice and a process, it becomes possible. Accepting our experience is big. Gaining the wisdom from it - HUGE. **I have watched as clients transform themselves in many ways — healing emotional strife, dis-ease, upheaval, as well as love and money woes.** Disease can awaken us to long held negative belief and emotion, and relationships are very instrumental in showing us where we need healing. We can overcome the mind-created challenge and go on to a much better life.

Spiritually speaking, everything and every experience is Divinely perfect. This is another life-altering perspective the Ego mind does not readily accept.

***

WHY YOU'RE HERE

It's very important to understand why you're here in this life in the first place.

Why do you believe you are here? Do you believe what you have been taught by society? Are you here to find a career, create friends and acquaintances, work and make money to buy a house? And then teach your children to do the same? Could life actually be that simple?

From a higher perspective, you are a being of God in the physical world, here to experience soul growth, expansion, joy and love! This can be done through amazing experiences with children, a career, friends, or a relationship, but the trick is not to lose the big picture in the doing. You are here to expand yourself, the overall consciousness of mankind and Universal Intelligence. Joy, health, and love are your default state of being.

That is right! Joy, love, and health is your true state of being. Beginning to live from that place is the miracle! Your patterned concepts, perceptions, thoughts, beliefs and your state of mind are the only thing stopping you from your joy!

When we can accept our experience as Divinely perfect, life begins with new peace and meaning. Our perception of life shifts to a flow of events for expansion. We learn, heal and transform ourselves. Each time we accept what is, we remove ourselves from any suffering and we take ownership of our own thoughts, and actions that brought us to where we stand. We may not like what is and seek to change, but by accepting what is we will never suffer again!

*That is a **miracle!***

- *We sabotage our own joy when we do not believe in our ability to create the life we desire.*

- *Relationships are instrumental in creating and revealing our beliefs and stories that limit our life.*

- *When we choose gratitude for the life we have, we claim our power.*

- *Our experience of life is perfect just as it is! Every occurrence, event, situation and conversation in life is in perfect Divine timing and shows up because we consciously or unconsciously believe it or desire it!*

- *Joy is your true state of being! Beginning to live from that place is the miracle! Your patterned concepts, perceptions, thoughts, beliefs and predominant state of mind are the only things stopping you from your joy!*

See Workbook for
Activities and Exercises

CHAPTER TAKEAWAYS

***

Coming
HOME

THE BIG AHA

It was the winter of 2002. Having spent the last few years expanding my ideas and perceptions of myself and life, I was learning to thrive. A budding property investor and just liberated from a restrictive corporate career, I decided to take a long-overdue vacation. I was free. I was excited. And I was so proud of myself for breaking free from a life I just could not tolerate any longer. My soul soared, my ego was petrified. I slept at night! I visited family in other states! I danced and partied! For the first time in more years than I could count, I sprang out of bed each day living life my way.

Then the news came.

As I was basking in the sunshine somewhere in the tropics, I received a call from the family doctor. My Mom was just diagnosed and admitted into the hospital. As usual and right on time, as soon as there was triumph and joy, something painful was lurking around the corner. My body craved the old painful feeling(s) and there I was in another opportunity to embrace a similar pattern of thought and feel the old and familiar feelings I had felt on and off, for most of my life.

Over the next 6 years I would exhibit some very unhealthy behavior. I chose to support my Mom in any way I could, which meant sharing my relatively new knowledge with her every chance I had, and by remaining at her side through her painful journey. As the disease progressed it would advance into her lymph system, her liver, her abdomen and finally conclude with ovarian cancer. The medical industry would proceed to poke, prod, slice, dice and take her through 3 horrific surgeries, a battery of 5 years of chemotherapy, radiation therapy, and it would end with her physician finally stating, "There is nothing else we can do," leaving just a shell of the person I once knew and loved. I watched it all in horror as my Mom struggled to recover her health again and again. Over the next six years, each of us would experience familiar times of sadness, discouragement, and anger. It became easy to see how we as humans, can blame circumstances, people, the career, the environment, for what we experience, and we both struggled. I understood it was not a good idea to jump in with negative thoughts and emotions, but I was angry. Angry because I was sure I had some information that would support my Mom and she would not hear it, and angry for what I believed at the time, life had done "to" my Mom.

During this period of my life I conducted a lot of research. I studied cancer, the treatments and the causes, food and nutrition, and the powerful mind. The most profound studies involved human behavior, how the mind effects our health and well-being, as well as the effect of continued chronic feelings on our life, and the devastating effect on the body. I became aware of the how and why we become discontent, discouraged and depressed. But the most amazing information came from my Mom, *three days after she left this earth.*

My Mom and I were very close throughout life. She did her best to love and support me when I was young and living in fear. She would surprise me with a new shirt I just had to have, a new album or a do dad for my bike. She was one of the few outspoken people that stood behind me when I decided to leave Corporate America. I looked out for her, helped her with the house, her finances, her car and finally, rarely left her side during chemotherapy. Although I was not aware of it at the time, I shared her discouragement and her discontent. Her resentment. I patterned her behavior. It was unhealthy behavior, yes. Today, I am acutely aware of this and if my Separate Self attempts to reaffirm an addictive State of Mind, I take ownership, refocus and choose differently. The resistance is released. At that time, neither one of us knew how to deal with our patterns and beliefs, and we re-affirmed our victimhood and pain through the events in our life. This day, the day she left this world, everything would shift for me and in a big way.

My Mom was gone. ***I was reeling.***

I watched a beautiful intelligent lady go through a lot of pain for years. To have her life end like this, enduring years of chemotherapy and surgeries, was difficult. The day she finally gave up, I was deeply saddened. I could not make any sense of the suffering. Now, it was time to make arrangements, and take all of the necessary steps to process the passing of someone I love. The legal forms and documents, the place for services, the right songs, the right pictures, the house to sell, the possessions to be looked at. One day while sitting on the couch with a close friend Katie, and overwhelmed with my current situation, in broad daylight, a beautiful and spectacular arrangement of light appeared. In an instant I could feel who it was. "It's my Mom!" I exclaimed to Katie. Katie's mouth dropped. I could not believe my eyes. I was shocked. How could I tell who it was? The feeling I had. The love I felt was that signature love of my Mom, amplified 1,000 times. It was the most amazing love I have ever felt. I was to my core, completely enthralled, excited and engulfed in a blanket of love I have never before experienced. My Mom began to speak, not with words, but with feeling. I could tell everything she was saying without the physical sound. "Michael, I am happy, I am no longer in pain." I was so put aback with what was happening I was scaring myself. She continued, "This was my journey. It's done. I am okay. I am happy." There was a pause as if I was supposed to speak, but I could not. She continued, " Now, I want you to live your journey and be happy." The love was so engulfing and so peaceful, and then the light faded and she was gone. I believe she could tell I was scared, so she faded. I never said a word to respond. It was so beautiful, it still affects me today. The love I felt that day was not the love we experience with the mind and body. The physical love we feel does not compare. What I felt that day was God Love. The Love we truly all are.

My Mom has been with me every step of the way ever since. For years, whenever I start down a path of damaging thought or behavior she will ring my left ear. She has always been with me. I don't know how it works, but I can tell you it has changed the course of my life.

Until this day, I was following a path that mirrored my parents. I had been happy, I had been sad. I lived without a real understanding of what life is and I wandered, making the best of it. This experience changed everything. That day I realized we don't die, but continue on. I realized our journey is perfect for each of us. I understood when I prayed or sought new learning I was heard. I understood *that love*, that place of love is where we end up after this life.

After I finished my worldly tasks with my Mom's affairs, I asked for the teacher that would show me what I needed to know. My next teachers would open up a whole new world for me. A profound understanding took over my life and enforced what I felt in my heart that day. I learned how amazing we really are, how the Ego Identity forms and how damaging our beliefs and patterns can be. From that day forward, I have sought to live from my heart, to watch my mind and love every moment of life as if it was perfect.

What a gift. **Thank you, Mom.**

***

HEAL – THE EGO ADDICTION

Each and every one of us has our own unique journey to the ultimate truth. Our soul chose to come here at this specific time because it believes there was something wonderful unfolding in the world that would facilitate the growth it yearned for. It does not matter how you experience it, through a family, a career, or a series of events. The important piece here, is to start listening to that *something greater* within you. Did I have any idea I would be doing this work? No. But, I could tell there was something pulling me away from my old experience. As I said, it started as a whisper and became a force I chose not to ignore.

There are so many situations, events and happenings in the world that I have become curious about. The positive gains in DNA research, mind and body empowerment, philanthropy, and technology vs. the negative, ugly, painful events, such as war, pestilence, 9-11; and now Covid 19. What could the deeper meaning be of seemingly negative or disastrous events? So many souls suffering or leaving the earth. From the events and situations in our own lives to worldly massive events - they are experiences to further raise the mass consciousness of mankind. From our trained and conditioned perspective it seems as though these negative events are disasters, which they absolutely are, but what was the result of these events? The perfect awakening of an entire new bonding experience of people across the globe.

A raising of consciousness.

AMERICA CHANGED.

The

WORLD CHANGED.

There is

LESS TOLERANCE OF HATE

and an expansion of

LOVE.

My masters have said on many occasions, "You are experiencing exactly what you wanted to experience Michael." I have come to understand that whatever energy, belief or story I hold in my consciousness, shows up in front of me. It may not be what I consciously want to experience but — consciously, or unconsciously — I experience it based on what I believe and feel to be true. Each mind has its own perspective and in the perfect journey, this is how we experience life.

Our soul ventures into the physical world at the best time to grow, transform and expand our consciousness. From this amazing journey of life and love and pursuit of higher truth, could those souls involved in positive or negative events have come here to have that experience? We are eternal, and we are choosing how and when we experience life, so is it so hard to believe?

We are not here to suffer. When we suffer, we are not appreciating our experience and instead choosing to react and resist! We are here to be joyful. To learn of our ability and power to create. Through our every experience, we are expanding the consciousness of the universe. As God and the universe expand through us and our experience we are contributing knowledge to infinite intelligence.

Through our thought and belief, we will create many experiences throughout life. We can choose to accept and take responsibility for our experiences and empower ourselves or we can hide from our own thought and creativity and unknowingly play a victim. When we evolve to be truly grateful for our life experience, a shift in our energy occurs and it will bring massive change to our life.

I have witnessed many clients heal themselves from illness and dis-ease by becoming aware of, and shifting, a predominant way of thought and repetitive emotion. Doctors and Neuroscientists have shown that chronic emotions and stress have a very negative effect on our physical body. And long term negative emotions such as resentment, anger, grief, and depression have a devastating effect on cell health. As we age, many of us become rigid in our perceptions and addicted to patterns of thought and the recurring emotional response. As our body and mind become conditioned to predominant states of mind, so do our cells and they reproduce with more receptors for our predominant states. This accelerates our aging so much so, that improved nutrition later in life can have little effect to improve our health. Revealing our addictive Separate Self and our reactive emotional states is very instrumental to return to our intended joyous life.

If we can understand how a drug addict becomes addicted to a drug and the resulting chemical rush felt in their body, then we can understand how we become addicted to thoughts and repetitive emotions from the chemical rush felt in our body. Both addictions affect the body/mind on a cellular level, and we are given multiple opportunities daily to reaffirm our familiar emotional state through the people and events in our lives. Over time we become stuck in a "comfort zone" of known and familiar thoughts and emotions as we become conditioned to feeling a certain way about people, work, food, money, love and life. Amazingly, I work with many people who actually become addicted to a life, a relationship, or a career they don't even like, and yet, do not change.

It's time to break the old bonds and create new intentions for your life! There are infinite possibilities to explore and that is what your life is about! Believe in your Essence as it guides and nudges you. Stop allowing your old pattern of, tomorrow will be a better day," and begin to think and feel differently.

When something horrible happens, many people tend to blame God. Again, God does not want us to suffer. God is Love. The love I felt when my Mom appeared in her Essence. The truth is, we all have free will. Our soul can poke us and cajole us to evolve, but can't make us do anything we choose not to do. If we decide to learn, we will learn, if we decide to change we will change. If we decide to choose joy and be happy, we will be happy!

*The truth is tragic events in our 3D world are caused by **many Egos.***

God does not create these events. These events are brought to the world by minds that judge, hate and believe they are right! Much wisdom is brought into conscious awareness from these events.

We could say that life is one big choice. We could say our soul chose to come here to experience our life and we chose what our major experiences would be. We always have a choice. Some lives are very mundane, we get the calling to change, to seek more, to become more, and the Ego and fear controls us — stops us in our tracks and we never reach our full potential. It seems all of us have a major fear or a major block in our lives. Some of us have many. Why? It's Divinely perfect and exactly what our soul wants to grow beyond.

And
BEYOND
that block lies
THE MAGIC.

Coming home is the process of undoing your stories, limiting thoughts and beliefs to become the amazing you. It is a choice to be free of, not good enough, knowing who you really are and why you are here. Coming home is loving yourself, embracing your courageous Essence, and living fully, beyond the conditioned ego and beyond the thoughts that control you.

God, the Universe and our Soul, do not control our Ego. We do. We always have free will. The direction of our life is our choice. There is nothing controlling our behavior or thought except ourselves. I suffered needlessly for years being so attached to the life I had made. At this time, I had no idea it would be so rewarding to let go of that current experience and embrace my heart's desire. I feared change and was functioning from the conditioning and beliefs of my separate self identity, the Ego, which lives in fear.

Are you ready to become
WHO YOU CAME HERE TO BE...
AUTHENTIC, FREE & COURAGEOUS?

It's high time we surrender and, "Let Go of The Sh*! Show." Give it up already. Much of what we have been taught, is just tradition, and generation after generation of old stories and beliefs!

Humanity is evolving, and much of what we are taught to believe is not true. We have false concepts about our abilities, and the purpose of our life. Throughout our younger years, we follow societies plan, seek happiness and love anyway we can get it, and are not taught how to understand and love ourselves. Many of us get caught up between temporary fulfillment and confusion. And we truly believe what we perceive in the world is real, even though it is created by an entire set of conditioned thoughts and beliefs.

We are part of an amazing adventure, an amazing experience for joy and growth. When we become vulnerable and humble, and seek fulfillment from within, from the highest part of us, life opens up to consistent joy, love and beauty. We become playful, and learn of our true ability and purpose here.

You are not separate from God! God is omnipotent and omniscient and is experiencing physical life through you. Your infinite self, your soul, wanted this physical experience! An experience of time and space! Let me say that again! Your soul, you, wanted this experience! If you step out of your Ego role in society for a moment and take a deeper look at your life, you are guiding yourself through an amazing and fun adventure and all the people and events in your life are actors and scenes in your play! They have the potential to mirror to you what it is you want to become aware of and evolve about yourself! If you trigger from an experience, an opportunity arises to reflect and shift a belief.

*It's time to wake up and **smell the coffee!***

In learning to create a conscious life, a conscious experience of growth and joy, we must choose to become aware of our thoughts and stories. Society, our job, our friends, the boss, our body, our hair, the house, the car, the children, social media, are all part of the fun adventure of life and can also keep us very distracted from a new and higher focus. Our energy is scattered. Many of us become so distracted and overwhelmed with our life, we tune out our real feelings. Our Ego has been hurt. We have emotional and physical addictions that keep us stuck in repetitive patterns. We have a known routine we follow that is predictable and we experience a predictable life. We react to the same events and challenges. When we tune into feelings and learn to feel our energy, our decisions and our surroundings, we are guided by intuition and we begin to listen to our soul.

When the soul speaks, our Divine essence is speaking and it speaks quietly, from a place of absolute peace. Meditation is a great way to attain a peaceful state and become receptive to our essence and the souls amazing wisdom. Being connected to Infinite intelligence, the soul guides us by asking, "What does the world want from me?" In contrast, the ego speaks abruptly and asks, "How can I get what I want?" The Separate Self Ego Identity does not believe life is working in our favor and can create great pain through expectation, attachment, judgment, and reactions to outcomes that differ from what it wants.

I am a huge advocate of creating a life that is all you want it to be! When you allow your heart and soul to guide you, your life will take exciting twists and turns and you will experience many amazing adventures! Letting go of my rigid ideas of life, while maintaining a focus on an end result has turned into a fun, over the top adventure. I have been all over the world, doing what I love most, by just being myself, and sharing the wisdom I have been given.

*The process begins with a **knowing**.*

Knowing, why you are here and what thought and belief is getting in the way of your absolute joy. Knowing, who you really are, transforming yourself. Allowing, thinking and living big – or what the Ego believes is big and the soul knows is possible and yours to experience. Being grateful daily for your journey. Letting go of the good and the bad and all the reasons why you tell yourself you can't.

Surrender, create intentions and follow your soul's calling. Never stop living fully. The gratitude and joy will overflow your life.

***

GETTING BEYOND OUR CHATTERING EGO MIND

One of the most effective ways I learned to experience an abundant, joyful life was through calming and refocusing the mind. I learned at a young age to be a thinker, an analyzer and a perfectionist to keep me out of trouble. As a result, my mind created a lot of stress. I have always thought that I could out think and figure out everything. Today, being in an entirely different state, the powerful answers I seek to life's challenges and experiences come without a lot of thought and little stress.

An extremely beneficial process to gain clarity, creativity and solutions while being at peace, is Meditation. What? You believe you don't have time to sit and be at peace? Ah, but you do! As your mind expands through this daily practice, you will experience beautiful insights, creativity and increased productivity. Start with 10 minutes a day the first 3 months. Find a quiet spot, set a timer and just close your eyes and relax your mind. If you have an overactive mind like mine, the meditation process will become invaluable and evolve to incredible visualization processes, brilliant answers to pressing questions and a profound connection to infinite possibilities.

I highly recommend it. Physically, stress levels fall and blood pressure drops. Mentally, you become very clear on what you can accomplish. Distractions are minimal. More importantly, it's a powerful connection to higher wisdom and your essence.

In the beginning it was a great way to calm myself and increase peace. Now it has become so much more. Done correctly, I have focused on healing a specific area of my body and without a proceedure, my body has healed itself! I have focused on experiences and the experience becomes my reality. During a meditation process, I have seen people's faces, and the next day the person is standing in front of me. It's amazing.

During my meditations I have learned to open up to my energetic connection with everything! And as I visualize in this state of peace, my daily focus becomes a very real part of my reality.

For the person who has a lot of hurt, anger or pain, meditation is the first step to a powerful and whole state, connecting the heart with the mind, beyond the Ego addictions and the Personal Identity.

Start today by finding your favorite spot in your home where you can be undisturbed for 10 minutes.

Close your eyes, get quiet and just focus on the three steps of your breath:

- *Focus on the breath coming in through the nose,*

- *then focus on the breath going out through your mouth.*

- *Then focus on the pause in between breaths and start again.*

Keep your focus on your breath. If your mind wanders, gently bring it back to the present and your breath, without judgment of your progress. There is no good and bad, remember? Let yourself breathe.

* * *

BECOMING WHOLE

When you truly understand yourself, and your purpose here without judgment, you can step into a place of power most of us struggle all our life to achieve. Through the ability to accept and appreciate your life and allow yourself to be authentic and genuine, joy will soar and you will attract amazing people and experiences, and interact with love, awareness and acceptance. As you adventure toward your end results, how others view you and what you accumulate become insignificant.

As you let go of the needy desire for recognition, or a huge bank account, through your daily intention and actions, it will appear! You can have, be or do anything you choose as long as you feel the joy, stay focused and believe in your perfect journey. This is the challenge you made for yourself.

The Separate Self Identity is our perfect teacher. As a youngster, many of us were taught to believe in limitations, doubts and imperfections. Being driven by the Ego desire, we become attached to and stressed over how we can attain our dream! And many of us stop believing it is possible! When we understand who we really are and let go of the "what can I get", or "what's in it for me" attitude, through our higher focus our desires are drawn to us without the pain and struggle. This is our empowered path. A path of trust. A trust that we are led in the direction to achieve our highest life. Through this trust, combined with a focus of the mind in meditation and visualization we become "at one" with our desire.

Why did I mention Science and Spirituality and the teaching that at our most basic level we are all one?

Let's review.

When we understand our oneness with everything
*we can **become one with anything.***

What the mind believes and feels to be true in this world becomes our experience. As we attain the peaceful state of meditation and visualize our dream, we are organizing and orchestrating the infinite possibilities of life and synchronicity's and serendipities begin to take place.

As we sync all of our energy, we become whole. Connecting the love of the heart and the focus of the mind, without distractions, we now direct all of our energy to one outcome. Flow and focus direct energy to support our highest desire, the world, and people, events and objects show up to support our path, without our old conditioned struggle.

The
CHOICE
is
YOURS.

You may pursue your dreams totally identified with what the mind believes you are, grappling with fears, judgments, attachments — thinking you are always gaining or losing something. Or you may pursue your dreams from your Divine Essence without attachment, without judgment, without fear and without wondering when the next upheaval will occur!

One word of caution.

Living from your Essence is an uncommonly beautiful way to pursue your dreams, your desires and to love the adventure of life! When you listen to the Soul speak and take action, you will be on the quickest, easiest path to your joy.

During my journey to fully understand my conditioned beliefs and thoughts, I became impatient. I desired to learn, change and move quickly beyond my dis-ease and challenges. The years on the roller coaster of happiness, and doubt, triumph, and fear, and the chattering Separate Self had became intolerable.

"Thinking" I had my patterned Ego mind under control, and my Essence was in charge of my reactions and thoughts *too soon* in this process, left me in a precarious place more than once.

During the journey to higher living, there were several times where I found myself on an amazing high. Feeling really great and being in a place where I thought, "Hey I've got this! It's no problem!," some old trigger, pattern or belief the Separate Self holds dear would come right back around and knock me off my high horse. This is to be expected. Give yourself the space to grow and integrate new thoughts and beliefs before claiming to be free of the old.

The Separate Self Ego can always pop up. Not to worry! We learn to recognize our old patterns and thoughts and the more we do, the more opportunity to shift them. Our Divine Essence will never trigger, never question or doubt, and is always in a state of peace, bliss and love. With time and acceptance we learn to hear and follow that voice.

Remember to honor your journey and be grateful for it. No matter how deep the old thought and belief may be, with awareness and a persistent new focus, your life will change. Let go of the Ego's need to "figure this out."

* * *

LIVE IN THE MIRACLE

Living in the Miracle, in Love, is not about, "Hey I've got this." Rather it is learning to love yourself and be yourself. Understanding you are an amazing and courageous being, requires no declaration.

For many of us, it is learning to unlearn what the mind has learned to believe. Learning to live in joy, to observe our Ego mind, smile and appreciate its presence.

(That in itself is a miracle!)

Living in the miracle transcends being "positive." Along with a positive focus, it is becoming aware of and honoring your connection with your world, the air you breathe, the water that flows, the soil that gives life. Each particle in each of these building blocks of matter, interacts with you and becomes a part of you. In the words of the ancients, you are not separate but one with all that is. Finding the wisdom in your adventure, will cultivate the ultimate trust in life. Positivity comes with this and so will everything else.

Know that your Divine Essence has no need to make declarations. You are magnificent and light. You are a miracle in physical form. You are Love. Your Essence does not need to prove anything.

Coming home is an adventure to becoming whole. A state of wholeness where we recognize the Highest Truth. You always have been whole, it's the Ego mind and all the doubts, fears, stories and challenges that believes you are not.

The secret to coming home is in finding real peace, flowing success and joy, and is in your discovery of this wholeness and knowing **you *are* everything to *have* everything.**

Today, my life is glorious. I love the work I do, the people I meet, the events, clients, my home, and travels. My sweetheart and I are beautifully in love. We watch our Ego carefully and do our best to stay in a heart space together. At times I still get triggered. Being responsible, I know it is another opportunity to evolve, and let go of an old emotional addictive/reactive way of walking through the world. So, I take the space to get curious, be grateful and expand my life.

*The only thing to **expand**, to **embrace**, to **embody** is this:*

ONLY LOVE IS REAL.

The Rest is
"PERFECTLY"
FROM YOUR EGO MIND.

When you begin to explore this wisdom in your life, new possibilities become evident. As you shift old belief and thought, old stories and experiences fall away. You will become less reactive and less fearful. You will experience a new life.

My advice is to re-read this book. Test the knowledge shared here. Allow yourself to integrate a new perspective. Get curious. Ask questions. Seek out a new teacher. Know your mind. Apply these steps. Watch your life become a miracle in motion. "Come Home" to peace, joy, and success. I wish you more understanding. I wish you love. I wish you great peace and bliss on your journey TO BECOME ONE WITH ALL YOU DESIRE!

*We are the problem and we are the **solution**.*